WEST OF WHEELING

WEST *of* WHEELING

HOW I QUIT MY JOB, BROKE THE LAW & BIKED TO A BETTER LIFE

JEFFREY TANENHAUS

HOUNDSTOOTH
PRESS

Cover design by Allison Tanenhaus & Derek George
Author photo by Josh New
Map illustration by Julia Emiliani

WEST OF WHEELING

How I Quit My Job, Broke the Law & Biked to a Better Life

ISBN   978-1-5445-2126-8 Hardcover
       978-1-5445-2125-1 Paperback
       978-1-5445-2124-4 Ebook

For Dad,
who gave me the love for travel.

For Mom,
who let me travel so long as I called.

CONTENTS

PART THREE: WINNING THE WEST

PART FOUR: CALIFORNIA AND BEYOND

The following is a true story, although names may have been changed. Events are described as they happened based on written notes, voice memos, and memory with rare exceptions made for narrative flow.

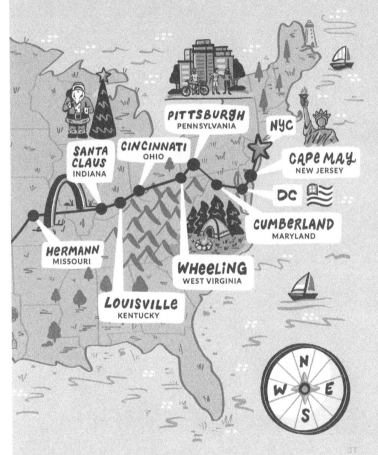

INTRODUCTION

When the fire alarm went off, nobody moved. Probably false. At work in Times Square, I was scrambling to meet a deadline. I didn't have time for drills.

A screaming fire truck pulled up outside. My coworkers at Red Carpet Events peered out the window and then went back to their desks. More sirens. The sound grew louder. Seven months' pregnant, an event operations manager called it a day just in case this wasn't a false alarm. Our graphic designer followed suit, but she didn't do much anyway. Rachel, the sales director, went out to investigate. The click-clack of high heels echoed down the hall. She returned a few minutes later, saying she smelled a little smoke. My fellow event developers began packing their bags, but not me. I couldn't go. My proposal wasn't done.

"Jeffrey, you're going to get Bianca everything she needs today, right?" Rachel asked, raising her voice above the noise and drumming her nails on the metal filing cabinet.

Yes, I needed to email the client by five. I couldn't evacuate now and come back later. I'd miss the Amtrak train for my dad's birthday upstate. We didn't use laptops or cloud software (still new in 2011), which made remote work impossible.

The building was on fire, but I was panicked about the time of day. The event planning agency was on the fourth floor. Worst case scenario, I could probably survive by jumping if they put a bouncy mat on the sidewalk.

Stop getting distracted, Jeffrey, I told myself. Everyone had bailed and I needed to focus on pricing out meeting space at the Metropolitan Club, down to bottles of mineral water. I locked the door so the flames and firefighters wouldn't reach me and stared at the spreadsheet with a clenched jaw and ringing ears.

This was my dream job.

Corporate event planning was stressful, but one thing made it bearable. My bike commute. After burning out at Red Carpet (which, fortunately, did not burn down), I worked for another company under similar pressure, but with none of the Times Square views. In fact, there weren't any windows at Elite 1 Events. Riding a Citi Bike to and from my new job was sometimes the only time of day I felt sunlight on my skin.

Citi Bikes are named after Citibank, which paid $41 million to brand NYC's bike sharing. The system launched in 2013 with 6,000 rental bikes that could get New Yorkers where they're going cheaper than a taxi and faster than the subway or bus.

Five thousand founding memberships sold out on the first day. I was #1387. The ninety-five-dollar yearly cost was less than a monthly pass on the subway. Annual users like me had forty-five minutes per trip before overtime fees kicked in. Returning the bike to any docking station reset the clock. One-way rides on equipment that you don't own, maintain, or store in a tiny apartment made bike share convenient and easy.

Most large American cities and colleges have similar programs. But bicycles for the masses—in this city? *Fuggedaboutit.* The press predicted mayhem and malfunction. They would be stolen, stripped for parts, and thrown into the river for fun. Broadway would run red with the blood of tourists wobbling around on two wheels. Blue bikes parked outside brownstones would ruin historic neighborhoods. Residents would revolt over lost parking. Docking racks would stymie first responders. Casualties from biking would pile up like garbage bags on the sidewalk.

None of that tabloid fearmongering came true. New Yorkers discovered the bikes saved time—the one thing we never have enough of. The bikes were wildly popular. Membership rose to one hundred thousand. People fought over the last bike like an empty taxi in the rain. Trips soared into the millions, then tens of millions. There was not a single fatality—not for four years, at least—a miracle considering pedestrians get mowed down in the crosswalk even with the light in their favor. Citi Biking was safer than city walking.

As soon as I tried Citi Bike I was hooked. Walking was too slow. The subway too crowded. While the masses were trapped underground, I exercised individuality outside. Moreover, my senses came alive. That fried noodle smell wafting through Chinatown. Arms turning to jelly biking over SoHo cobblestones. Afternoon sunshine warming my skin along the Hudson River Greenway.

Each ride was an adventure. Biking in the city was like being in a video game but playing with real life. Consequences mattered, but so did the rewards. Every weekday I faced the same obstacle course, but the dangers popped up in new places: shopping carts full of cans, double-parked delivery trucks, taxis turning across the bike lane without yielding. Sure, there were pitfalls—and plenty of potholes—but rather than rely on the subway or bus, I was moving at my own speed. I was in control of the rhythm and route. No waiting, no transfers, no delays. Self-propelled power was addictive, especially in the world's most exhilarating city.

My commute began near DUMBO by selecting a bike docked two blocks from my apartment in RAMBO, one of the few neighborhood acronyms that didn't catch on. Minutes later I was huffing and puffing up the Manhattan Bridge, which fed me into Chinatown where I cruised up Allen Street past tenements, restaurants, and bars on the Lower East Side.

More commuters joined the bike wave surging up the protected lane on First Avenue. After avoiding jaywalking doctors and nurses on Medical Mile, a left onto Thirty-Ninth Street led me into the heart of traffic-clogged Midtown. I docked the bike on Broadway just south of Times Square, five miles and forty minutes since leaving Brooklyn.

My workplace on Fortieth Street felt like a holdover from the bad old days when drugs and smut ruled Times Square. Ahead on Eighth Avenue loomed the Port Authority, a bus terminal that comedian John Oliver called "the single worst place on planet Earth." Across the street from our office was a store with neon lights advertising XXX DVDs, adult toys, girls, a male room, and something called "buddy booths."

Our building was wrapped in dirty tinted glass. The stairwell reeked of pot from the recording studio above and sewage from whatever was below. I used the back door through accounting, a one-woman department that doubled as human resources. I'd often find Margaret hunched over some files. She'd turn and chirp, "Good morning," pushing up oversized glasses. In her sixties, she lived alone uptown with two ailing dogs.

I pulled a Clark Kent inside a storage closet stacked with candleholders and linen samples, changing from bike sweats into business casual. I was energized for any task, but drowsiness soon numbed my brain. Not because pedaling tired me. Just the opposite.

I worked in "The Grotto." Our back office had no natural

light. The marketing manager and I taped over the light switch, using desk lamps to set the mood.

Winter was the worst. Not because it was cold—I could layer for that. But because the morning bike commute was the only time to feel daylight. The sun would set by five, and we weren't allowed to leave before six, even if we had finished everything. When I stayed later, Margaret and I were often the last two working. She also acted as my part-time therapist. On my way out, I'd lean on the doorframe with one foot crossed over the other, helmet tucked under my arm. Margaret would push back her rollie chair with a sigh and spill the office drama *du jour*.

Job security was a big concern. Consultants had been hired: a husband-and-wife duo named Andy and Andrea. We called them "The Andys." Margaret knew she was on thin ice, but couldn't afford to retire. Only the two principals had been there longer. I wasn't in their long-term plans either, but I was versatile enough to jump from sales and marketing to project management as the agency expanded and contracted with guidance from The Andys.

"OK, Jeffrey, maybe you can take me through what you do here," the male Andy said one morning, standing behind me as my fingers trembled scrolling through a proposal for a themed music festival on Governors Island. Andy's coffee breath raised the hairs on my neck and twitched the hairs in my nose.

A week later, the company president called a "family meeting." We circled up in nervous anticipation. He fired the marketing manager in front of everyone. The six-foot-five former minor league baseball pitcher held back tears saying goodbye. I assumed his marketing role and kept my desk organized as if any day could be my last.

Our company's growing pains were painful, yet without growth. We only numbered a dozen employees at any time. In two years, I saw eleven people leave. I would be the twelfth. "Elite 1, where no one sticks around!" was an inside joke.

I uncrossed my feet and put on my helmet. Time to hit the road.

"You be careful, guy!" Margaret called after me in her native Texas twang.

Getting home by my own effort was more measurable and satisfying than any project that day. On a bike, I was working for myself and focused on the present. I didn't have time to think about failures of the past and insecurity of the future. I was floating through my mid-thirties without a stable job, mortgage, or child to ground me. I could go anywhere. What sounded like a dream to some was an existential crisis to me. Friends were on their second kid, home, or spouse. I was on my second failed job in events. I couldn't shake the feeling that I was losing at life.

Citi Biking turned the pain of inadequacy into progress that felt good. So good that I wanted to keep biking—across America and on this very same equipment. I've always been curious about the world; I even majored in geography. But despite a global metropolis like New York City, where I lived with plenty of privilege, I felt sheltered from reality and tied to a desk in the dark.

I want to know the real America—its past and present—one backroads mile at a time. I want to feel the sun on my skin. I want to immerse myself in national parks and historic sites. I want to meet different people and make new friends. Most of all, I want to find a more comfortable city to call home. One where I feel in control of my future and can work on projects I genuinely care about.

I'm ready to explore life in a slower lane. My cross-country Citi Bike dream has no precedent, but I'd rather pedal ahead than sink in self-pity, even if my destiny is more uncertain than ever.

Part One

THIS LIFE
I LEAVE

*"I honestly think it is better to be a
failure at something you love than to be
a success at something you hate."*

—George Burns

CHAPTER 1

ESCAPE FROM NEW YORK

Where the hell you going with *that?*"

The captain is blocking my path on board. A white shirt stretches over his puffed chest. Biceps flex like cannonballs. A seagull shrieks and flies away. The air is thick with tension like before a duel in an old Western. But I'm not in a dusty frontier town. I'm on the edge of Manhattan taking a ferry to New Jersey.

I pretend that my baggage isn't out of the ordinary. Nothing to see here, folks, just a nice day to hit the Shore with my bike, which isn't really mine. It's a rental Citi Bike. It can't leave the city.

The sun is packing high-noon heat at 9:00 a.m. It feels like one of those August Fridays when people take a long lunch and never return to the office, ending up on a restaurant patio packed with tables and chatter. Phones vibrate with work emails, but attention fades with every sip of refreshment. Weekend vibes take over.

The attitude on summer Fridays at Elite 1 was mercifully on this same wavelength. We got out early at 3:00 p.m. Otherwise, we worked from nine to six without a break. Lunch culture was grabbing a sandwich to eat at our desks in a windowless room, pecking away at projects and brushing crumbs off the keyboard. So at three o'clock on summer Fridays, I'd skip down the stairs and throw up my hands in delight. Sunshine. Air. Freedom. Monday morning seemed so far away.

What if I had a life where I looked forward to Monday? I'd been thinking about taking a Citi Bike across America for more than a year, and today I'm turning those thoughts into action. I'm launching myself into uncharted waters to see what else is out there. Nobody has tried leaving NYC quite like this.

Suddenly I miss the security of a routine. At 3:00 p.m. on Fridays, I'd Citi Bike down the Hudson River Greenway to yoga in Tribeca to de-stress from the week. At three this Friday, I could be doing poses for a mugshot. What happens now determines how far I'll get on my journey. California is the goal, but I'll settle for safe passage to New Jersey.

The captain calls my bluff. He's built like a statue and stands stone-faced with bronzed skin. He demands to know why I'm taking this bike on the boat. The waves quiet down to hear what I have to say. Oh God, where do I start?

"Hey man, relax, just a day trip to the Shore...I'm coming back later," I say with a smile.

Silence.

"Are you *kidding* me?"

"No, I am coming back later," I insist. I have evidence. "I'm an annual member. See, here's my key."

"These bikes can't go to Jersey. No-ho way," he howls.

"I...I'm just...going for...for the day." Choking on my own lie, I fumble for words.

The captain's tattooed forearm swings forward. He grabs the handlebar. "That's grand larceny," he barks.

"No...no, you don't understand, I—"

"I'm calling the cops!"

Worst case scenario. I always brace for it. Expecting the worst helps me avoid disappointment, but not since jumping out of a burning building has my worst-case scenario been as bad as getting arrested.

Thankfully, I'm not. None of the doom swirling around my mind is happening in real life. There is no burly boat captain. The ticket taker is a skinny guy with spotty skin who has no reaction as I roll the bike aboard. Nobody says a word. Nobody calls the police. Nobody cares. It's New York. It's summer. It's Friday.

A horn blasts and motors gurgle. Relief at making it on board turns into stress about getting off. What if I'm arrested in...New Jersey? Yes, that's it. I'm going to get arrested upon landfall. The story will go viral. My name will be smeared online. I'll never get a desk job again. My nerves shoot higher than Manhattan skyscrapers. I'm on a ferry to New Jersey with a bicycle that belongs in New York.

I tie the bike to a railing with a bungee cord and go up to the top deck. The best views of Manhattan are when you leave it. So many tall buildings so close together gives me goosebumps. The sun shines off the crown of the Chrysler Building and catches my eye. Its pointed elegance and crafty construction make it my favorite.

During the height of the skyscraper race in 1929, the Chrysler Building was locked in competition with a bank at 40 Wall Street. The drama was personal. Two former architectural partners were trying to build the world's tallest building in the same city at the same time. When the Chrysler Building's architect released plans showing its height, construction on 40 Wall Street stopped a little higher—certain victory was theirs. But a secret spire made inside the Chrysler Building was later hoisted into place, making it the tallest manmade structure on Earth. The next day, the stock market crashed and the Great Depression began.

Learning about history helps me appreciate New York beyond the vibrant bars and delicious, diverse restaurants that make living in an expensive city worth it. History is free. These fascinating stories of the past motivated me to become a tour guide. When I should have been going to grad school or climbing the corporate ladder, I spent three years atop red double-decker buses.

The route stayed the same, but the tourists changed. I always asked where they were from. I met people from across the US coming to the Big Apple for the first time. Now I am leaving my home for theirs: Ohio, Missouri, Oklahoma, New Mexico. I've never been to Columbus, St. Louis, Tulsa, or Albuquerque. Will I be welcomed with the same kindness as I showed them?

Tour guiding wasn't the corporate career I envisioned after graduating from Dartmouth. It was a gig I got good at and stayed with for too long, but it led to a San Francisco startup asking me to collaborate on a travel app. That was during the app gold rush in 2009. *New York City Essential Guide* would become a top fifty travel app for iOS. Even better, the app got me a job that sounded like a dream: to plan events at exclusive restaurants, luxury hotels, and landmarks like the Statue of Liberty and Metropolitan Museum of Art.

Before the Andys and the windowless grotto at Elite 1 Events, I worked for Red Carpet Events with postcard views of Times Square. The work was grueling, but the perks were fabulous. I balanced offers of free meals at steakhouses with industry events at The Plaza Hotel, the New York Stock Exchange, and the newest rooftop bar. As a tour guide, I only knew the city from the street. Now I was an insider.

I moved from my childhood bedroom in the suburbs to a glassy building in downtown Brooklyn. My studio had a terrace with views of lower Manhattan. My office overlooked the glowing heart of Times Square. Finally, my career was off to a promising start. I felt on top of New York.

The honeymoon didn't last long. Working at Red Carpet was like juggling cannonballs on a treadmill. I came early, stayed late, and ate lunch at my desk, but there was never enough time in the day. Sometimes I ordered delivery from across the street because I couldn't afford a quick break to grab food myself.

When the iPhone's alarm clock snapped me awake each morning, I instinctively checked work email with bleary eyes. I felt gastric acids percolating into my intestines before I even got out of bed. This stress eventually triggered my ulcerative colitis out of remission and into a health crisis. I had been diagnosed with the disease as a teenager. Six pills a day kept it in check, but now taking nine wasn't enough.

One Sunday evening I stopped by the office. I had a busy week ahead. I didn't plan to stay more than an hour or two, but it was my first time working with double commissions. I was pulling my hair out. Then a spontaneous celebration erupted in Times Square. Osama bin Laden had been killed. People gathered to honk and chant, "U-S-A! U-S-A!" Fire trucks with flashing lights joined them, but not me. I didn't leave until 3:00 a.m.

As the only one in the office who spoke Spanish, I was once on the phone helping a client in Mexico City while my boss, Rachel, berated me in English from across the room about a different event. The director of sales wore sharp outfits and was a pro at winning business. Seven years my senior, Rachel was also single and Jewish. The president of the company liked to joke that we should couple up.

The Mexico City client was coming for a site visit and would arrive Saturday. Rachel ordered me to set up dinner for them at The Sea Grill in Rockefeller Center. I called our contact to reserve a table next to the ice skating rink. I wasn't invited until the client asked Rachel why I wasn't attending. I love seafood and was eager to dine at an upscale restaurant, even though it was for work on a weekend.

As the entrees arrived, Rachel opened our proposal and got down to business. I took out my copy to take notes, moving sea scallops and truffle mashed potatoes out of the way. By the end of the meal, my pen was running out of ink. I thought this would be a social outing with a side of business, not a Saturday night work session.

Outside, we said good night to the client. I then turned to Rachel to ask what she was up to. Flashing a clenched smile, she said, "I just need to get this cab. And you need to get to work. I expect those changes first thing Monday." The next yellow taxi stopped, and she slipped inside without looking back. I walked to the office alone.

As work anxiety deepened, my disease worsened. Industry parties and free sea scallops weren't worth bleeding into the toilet. I quit my dream job to freelance.

The first expense to cut was a $104 monthly MetroCard. To replace the subway, I bought a used Raleigh for $300 from a bike shop under the BQE. Citi Bike hadn't been invented yet. Aside from a beach cruiser on vacation, I hadn't been on a bicycle since I was a kid. I felt unsteady at first. The tires were too narrow. I had never ridden a road bike.

My first ride was over the Manhattan Bridge to Manhattan and then across the Brooklyn Bridge back to Brooklyn. What a perspective! On a bike, I felt like I was in a new city. On days when I felt sad or lonely, I hopped on the bike to explore. I pedaled twenty miles roundtrip for a hot dog at Nathan's Famous in Coney Island or fried galamah (calamari) at Randazzo's in Sheepshead Bay. Getting from A to B ended in a feeling of accomplishment that I never got at work.

Off the bike, life wasn't so good. I stopped paying for transport and dining out, but was burning through savings to cover rent and health insurance. Freelance tour guiding wasn't enough, nor was app income once the developers and Apple took their bites. After almost a year on my own, my savings were nearly gone. I needed to get a full-time job and fast.

I attended an industry party hosted by my old employer, Red Carpet. I indulged in free booze and networked without inhibition. I chatted with the VP of Elite 1 Events who knew me from my time at Red Carpet. It just so happened he needed a junior business development manager. I started work a few weeks later.

This was a great chance to restart my career with an attentive mentor—one who wouldn't ditch me after dinner. But Elite 1's corporate services were a tough sell. Our flowery logo looked like we planned weddings. Our website had photos of extravagant parties like a pirate's treasure dinner on a beach in Bermuda. Who was going to hire us to run a conference in Midtown? Worst of all was the lack of natural light in The Grotto. Even jail cells have little windows. The best part of this job was Citi Biking home. When the company lost its biggest client, I agreed to leave three months later after my last event.

The timing worked out. My apartment lease expired two months before my job ended. I boxed everything into a five-by-seven storage unit. The door barely closed because of that Raleigh bike, which I almost sold to make room and money. I hardly used it with the ease and prevalence of Citi Bike. I had the storage unit in Brooklyn and opened a post office box in Chinatown, but was left with nowhere to sleep.

For two months I bounced around couches, dog sat, or paid for the cheapest Airbnb within walking distance of a Citi Bike station. Sometimes I didn't know where I would sleep that night. I wore the same pair of jeans and kept a backpack with some shirts, underwear, and toiletries. I was an urban nomad on a bicycle.

To me, Citi Bike was stability. Riding its sturdy frame gave me comfort and control when I felt down on my luck. Five years after finding my dream job and apartment, I no longer had either. I needed a restart and not in event planning or in New York. My annual bike pass was set to expire hours after getting on this ferry. Rather than renew and continue to struggle here, I resolved to buy the bike and see what life was like beyond the boroughs.

Williamsburg. Manhattan. Brooklyn. The ferry passes under the trio of East River bridges whose bike lanes I know so well. Bike lanes make me feel safe. Their lines give me guidance. I'm a rule follower and an introvert. My high school GPA was 3.99 out of 4, yet I rarely spoke in class even if I knew the answer. My lowest grade in college was one single B in math, my academic kryptonite. My numbers in adulthood are nearly perfect too. I pay bills in full and on time, every time. My credit score is above 800. I avoid conflict and stay out of trouble. I've never been arrested or pulled over by police. No tickets or fines, except an overdue Scarsdale Public Library book during my non-rebellious youth in the suburbs. Following the rules as an adult makes me feel grounded, just like getting good grades did as a kid.

Being a goody-goody ends today. I'm breaking bike share terms of service and crossing state lines with property worth more than one thousand dollars. Grand larceny is a felony. Consequences are stronger than a B in math. My shoulder angel is hopping mad, but I tell it to calm down.

Back when this idea was a pipe dream, I asked Citi Bike for permission and was laughed off the phone. Follow-up emails were ignored. I even upgraded my LinkedIn account to message marketing execs at Citibank and outdoor brands about collaboration and sponsorship. No response. So just like Sinatra sang, I'll do it *My Way* and pay $1,200 for the bike. That's the maximum overtime fee, which was billed to my membership-linked credit card. Citi Bike took my money, so I bought their bike.

(Maybe Citi Bike wouldn't mind. In 2015, the year I departed, the company made $5.2 million just from overtime fees.)

Of course I could get a proper touring bike for less, but I wanted to find purpose and explore America on the same trusty equipment that empowered me in NYC. I banked more than $6,000 after giving up my apartment and crashing with friends while working the last two months of my job. I've saved for this. In my mind it feels a little wrong, but in my heart it feels just right.

I lean into the breeze. The World Trade Center pierces the sky. The Statue of Liberty salutes the sun. I wave her goodbye and flick my shoulder angel into the wake leading back to the island where I was born. We pass under the Verrazzano Bridge, and New York Harbor becomes a watery desert. This bike on a boat looks out of place. Is it nervous like I am? I turn to catch a last look at the skyline and tear up. The buildings are shrinking. I don't know when I'll be back or what lies ahead.

Laughter breaks my thoughts. Two guys are joking around. The sun is out and the sky is blue. People on board have beach chairs and straw mats. They're relaxed and ready to start the weekend early on this summer Friday. Their worries can wait until Monday but mine cannot. The captain cuts the motor and the boat bumps into the dock. New Jersey. Everyone gets off except for me. I'm stuck to the seat thinking about the worst-case scenario. I'm about to find out what happens when a Citi Bike leaves the city.

CHAPTER 2

BREAKAWAY

"Here, lemme help you," says a crew member walking toward me with a smile. "The captain was like, 'I just want that Citi Bike off my boat!'"

OK, so the boat people noticed. I was worried they would call the police. Instead, they are helping me carry out my plan. I untie the Citi Bike from the railing while the crew wheels my bike trailer down the gangway.

My trailer has two wheels like a hand truck. It's made by Burley, a company known for bike trailers that tow kids or dogs. Touring cyclists without live cargo prefer panniers, or saddlebags, that go over the wheels. The bags attach to bolts on the bike frame, but a Citi Bike doesn't have that. It's meant for short trips with a basket for a backpack or purse. I need more space. Burley's trailer has a swivel arm that clips onto the seat pole, making it compatible with any bike.

I packed light—maybe too light. A few white tees from Uniqlo. Four pairs of underwear. Faded gym shorts and old blue running shoes that match the bike. To dress up, I have one long-sleeved shirt and a pair of quick-dry pants. I wear six-dollar sunglasses from CVS and half-finger Nike gloves from a soccer player Halloween costume seven years ago. The bike was so expensive that I didn't invest in clothing or equipment. I dreamed of buying a drone but settled for a selfie stick. I have simple toiletries and extra sunscreen. I won't be far from food, so I only carry protein bars and trail mix from Trader Joe's. For camping, I bought the cheapest one-person tent and sleeping bag at Walmart. No bike tools or tubes, but I can wave for help with a yellow smiley face flag taken from the storage closet at my last job. Touring experts might not give me one week in the wild.

On shore, people line up for the boat back to Manhattan. Everyone is staring at me, the last one off. "Well, look at that. I don't think you're supposed to take a Citi Bike out here," mutters a woman to her friend.

I walk faster, eyes down and jaw clenched. In the parking lot, I prop the kickstand and take out blue painter's tape to cover Citibank's logo. They're not sponsoring me, and I'm in uncharted territory with this thing. I want to make the bike less conspicuous.

A car pulls up and the window rolls down. I brace for a citizen's arrest.

"Nice day for a ride! You know how to get to the path to Highlands?" asks the guy behind the wheel.

Wait, is someone else trying to help me? I'm aware of a bike path, but my focus is on the tape and not Google Maps, which I'm trusting to navigate me across the country, just as soon as I cover these corporate logos. The driver points to a waterfront path called the Henry Hudson Bike Trail that will kick off my ride—the first yellow bricks on a long-ass road to the Golden State.

I walk the bike on the sidewalk thinking it will look less out of place than riding it. Two women walk toward me. I pull over on the grass and pretend to check my phone. My heart and mind are racing and my body is paralyzed. I'm never going to make it to California, much less down the Jersey Shore, if I hide every time I see someone. Get on the fucking bike, Jeffrey! Start riding and stop being afraid.

The familiar whirl of the spokes softens my heartbeat. My butt sinks into the cushy seat. It feels just like riding in New York except for the drag of the trailer and the skyscrapers seen from a new state. I've made landfall in New Jersey one month before Citi Bike would expand across the river to Jersey City.

The paved path turns to dirt. Muddy puddles and exposed roots are the first taste of off-road life beyond the Manhattan grid. A yellow sign with a black diamond warns, "Caution: Primitive trail with obstructions and uneven surfaces. For use by hardy experienced hikers, equestrians, and all-terrain cyclists." Jesus, I've gone less than a mile and I'm already at the mercy of nature.

The trail empties onto a residential street. "Goooood morning, New Jersey! So nice to be here. Thanks for coming out, yous guys!" I chuckle at my welcoming committee of trash and recycling bins at the bottom of each driveway. I'm in Highlands, a name I don't think about until I turn onto Miller Street and grind to a stop. My first hill. High land.

Living in Brooklyn, I'd ride to work over the Manhattan Bridge and count the bikes I passed. The average road bike weighs seventeen to twenty pounds. A Citi Bike? Almost forty-five. The bridge's bike path was so steep that riding a Citi Bike felt like pedaling a couch. Gears make hills easier. A common road bike has twenty-seven. Citi Bike? Just three: slow, slower, and slowest. Yet I could Citi Bike up the bridge while sitting down and pass cyclists on road bikes. I looked effortless. I felt their dismay and ate it for breakfast. It wasn't a race, but in New York, competition creeps into everything.

Now in New Jersey, I'm competing with myself and pulling

forty extra pounds with the trailer. How the hell am I going to cross America if I'm walking up the very first hill? At the top, I hop on and pedal toward the Atlantic Ocean. I'm going east. This is where I'm from. The watery horizon is a blank slate to project my dreams, but nothing comes to mind. I need to go west and figure out what these dreams are. And the best way to bike west from NYC is to go south down the Jersey Shore where it's flat and safer for bikes.

Sandy Hook peninsula is to the north. Beyond it, tiny Manhattan skyscrapers shimmer like a mirage. I swallow hard. I'm ready to see America. I'm ready to meet new people and, eventually, find the future me. I turn the handlebars south and glide down a ramp. The Jersey Shore unfolds before me, baking in the hazy sunshine. I see sand. I smell ocean. I taste freedom.

BLLAAAM! blares a horn behind me. Friday traffic to the Shore is to be expected, but the narrow shoulder pitted with storm drains is not. The trailer is wider than the bike and I'm still not used to it. Cars are trying to pass. I have to move over.

Suddenly, the drain grabs a wheel and the trailer flips over. The drag yanks me back, almost throwing me off the seat. I hit the brakes and keep balanced, but the damage is done. The trailer's yellow rain cover, which doubles as a warning to cars behind me, is ripped. My nerves are frayed, but I'm powering through my first morning on a mix of adrenaline, anxiety, sunshine, sea breeze, and Jersey geography.

Sea Bright...Monmouth Beach...Long Branch...Deal...Asbury Park. The Shore towns are rolling by. I don't even take a sip of water until Deal, where oceanfront mansions stop me in my tracks. I haven't eaten anything today. I look inside the trailer for a chocolate chip protein bar. The snack makes me feel sleepy.

Last night was rough. I only got two hours of rest. My original plan was to rise early this morning and pick the perfect specimen before commuters plucked bikes from the racks. It would be an intense trial and error just before I made my escape by ferry. The upside was that by the time Citi Bike knew one of their blue babies was missing on a Friday afternoon, I'd be in New Jersey. Maybe they'd wait until Monday to call me. Maybe then I'd be in Delaware.

But last night, the bike sharing gods left me a gift under the Queensboro Bridge. I went out for Mexican and margaritas with a friend and her parents on the Upper East Side. My last supper, they joked. After dinner, at the bike rack under the bridge, I spotted a new model. This summer Citi Bike was rolling out version 2.0 with a sleek rear fender and taillight.

The bike felt great! At every red light going down Second Avenue, I hopped off to look closer. This wasn't just a new model bike, but a *new* new model bike. The spokes sparkled. The frame had no scratches. Waiting for the light at Forty-Second Street, I wondered, "Is this The Bike?" By Thirty-Fourth Street I knew. At Twentieth Street I docked. I was spending my final night with my best friend Tommy in Stuyvesant Town. Off the clock, I inspected the bike like crazy. Even the bell worked. (The bells never work.)

In The City That Never Sleeps, this bike might be gone come dawn. As I thought about what to do, a woman slammed her bike into the dock. She then gracefully lifted her purse from the basket and began walking in my direction. I felt an overwhelming urge to say something, but in New York you don't talk to strangers.

"Uhh...excuse me," I trembled as I broke social norms.

She paused under the streetlight. A tiara held back shoulder-length blonde hair. Her nose was thin. Cheekbones round and shiny. She looked like a middle-aged Alice in Wonderland.

"What if I were to tell you that I'm going to ride this bike cross-country tomorrow."

One sandal began tapping the sidewalk as her calves flexed silently.

"Well, that's gonna cost a fortune. And I don't think the bike is going to make it that far. They can barely make it to Central Park," she said, smiling widely. Her teeth glowed like the Cheshire Cat in Disney's animation. "I mean, it's a great idea. I love the idea. But which way will you go? And how far are you gonna get?"

"I don't know," I replied. "But I wanna try. I've been thinking about this for so long that I just have to do it, but I'm scared."

"When you get that feeling of fear, it means you're doing something right," she offered.

"Really? I—I'm prepared to pay the $1,200 fee," I explained. "I've read the fine print of what happens if you don't return a bike. I've budgeted for that. I'm just worried about the legal consequences."

"I work for a law firm," Cathie stated, introducing herself. "Boutique firm on Broadway and Fifty-Third. Seven of them, really good lawyers."

I love New York. Just when I needed a lawyer in my corner, I met one on the corner.

"That's great! What kind of law do you practice?"

"Oh, I'm not a lawyer. I'm the receptionist!" she laughed. "Everyone knows me as the lady who bikes. I bike everywhere! At lunch, I Citi Bike around Central Park. I don't know if I'd go to work without riding a Citi Bike. It's all I ride."

Exactly! That's why I quit my job and wanted to keep riding. Cathie got it. We were exchanging Instagram handles when headlights beamed onto us. My first thought was, "Oh God, the police are after me." Then I remembered I hadn't taken the bike yet.

A man got out of the truck, a tanker with some kind of hose, and started spraying. I'd never seen bike-wash trucks. Maybe it was pesticide for West Nile mosquitoes? Cathie walked away backward, watching me while receding into the darkness. The headlights kept shining as the spraying got closer. I needed to make a fast decision. I inserted my membership key. The dock light flashed green, and with a chime, released bike #11100 for the very last time.

Avon-by-the-Sea...Shark River...Belmar...Spring Lake...Sea Girt...Manasquan...Brielle. In Point Pleasant Beach, Broadway sparkles like it's paved with tiny diamonds. Broken glass everywhere has me fearing for the tires. Then my phone vibrates with a 718 area code. Brooklyn. Citi Bike is based in Brooklyn. They probably want to chat about why one of their bikes is moving toward Mantoloking. Send to voicemail.

Ocean Avenue is alive with carnival rides and mini golf. Motels have no vacancy. The breeze smells like cotton candy. The screams of delighted children contrast to my worry over broken glass. I stop at an empty beachfront lot, no doubt a victim of Hurricane Sandy three years ago. I need to check that message. I raise the phone to my ear. An annoying but familiar voice speaks quickly. It's that magazine sales rep who calls every few months to ask me to buy advertising for my app like it's the first time he's ever called. I've never been so happy to hear from him. I delete the message and bike on, the trailer feeling twenty pounds lighter.

The three o'clock sun is burning bright. This was the magic hour on summer Fridays when I'd get out of work early and bike down the Hudson River path to yoga in Tribeca. An hour of chaturangas and warrior twos cleansed me from the week's drama. Two full days separated me from going back to that office again.

Now in Mantoloking, I am freer than ever, yet feeling trapped like on a Monday morning. Adrenaline is wearing off.

My legs hurt. I'm hungry. I want to dock this bike and begin the weekend with yoga and a nap. But my comfy mattress is in storage and all I've got is a thin sleeping bag and a small tent. Is it too soon to quit and turn around? Biker's remorse is a real thing.

A new voice gets me back on track. It's Google Maps telling me to turn left and my destination is on the right. It's not California, but who cares. I've made it to Lavallette. Tonight I'm crashing in the backyard of a host on Warmshowers.org, a social network like Couchsurfing but for cyclists. The homeowners are in Pennsylvania on a weekend ride. I have permission to camp in their backyard, which is a disappointing mix of cracked concrete and pebbles. I pitch a tent on their wood deck instead. A solar-heated outdoor shower washes anxiety down the drain. There is no toilet, so I walk a few blocks to public tennis courts to use a porta-potty.

After thirty-eight miles of asphalt, I'm ready to feel some sand. With the five o'clock shadow I move onto the beach. I'm by myself watching waves break on shore, a gentle rhythm similar to pedaling. Then I remember...I forgot the bike!

Tradition dictates that cross-country cyclists dip their back wheel in the ocean of departure. Do I really need to do this? I'm already doing everything wrong. I'm wearing gym clothes and old sneakers, not padded Lycra shorts and those clip pedal things. I track mileage on Google, not Garmin. And I'm on a freaking Citi Bike. It's locked to the deck at the house. I'm too tired to get it or even dip a toe in the water. I walk back barefoot and prepare for my first night on the road and under the stars.

---- **CHAPTER 3** ----

DOWN THE JERSEY SHORE

My eyes open to a pale blue wall. Waking up with the sky as your ceiling feels so natural. Then I remember how I got here. My legs, my butt...are you sore? I wiggle out of the tent on my stomach, knocking over a potted plant with my foot. I stand up slowly, ready to wince, but the pain never comes. It's like yesterday never happened until I see that blue bike. It's just where I left it, waiting for a rider. I shake my head and laugh. This is my Citi Bike now. I am its one and only rider. I will call it Countri Bike.

I pedal toward Toms River, the seat of Ocean County and home to the 1998 Little League World Series champs. That was the year I graduated from high school. Like most of my classmates, I got my license at sixteen and started driving to school. Juniors used a gravel lot. Seniors parked on pavement outside the cafeteria where the cool kids would steal a smoke. Like cigarettes, cars were a symbol of independence, a vehicle into adulthood. Bicycles were for children.

Right now I'm on a bicycle and feeling scared like a lost child. The safety of the shoulder disappears leading to the Thomas A. Mathis Bridge. A narrow ledge gives marginal refuge from the woosh of speeding cars. It's a summer Saturday, and I'm sure more than a few carefree New Jersey teens are behind the wheel. The trailer barely fits on the ledge, which sparkles like a kaleidoscope of broken glass and taillights. I shuffle sideways pulling the bike and praying that a side mirror doesn't send my body tumbling into Toms River. It's not a joke. Death is waiting for me down there.

High on a bridge with a low railing, I feel the danger of navigating a motor vehicle's world without one. Yet I can improve my chances of survival. Today I debut a yellow vest with reflective stripes. It makes me look like a school crossing guard, but the neon screams, "I'm here. I'm human. Don't hit me!" Bright and baggy, this vest is my cheapest and most comforting accessory.

I clear the bridge and ride residential streets into downtown Toms River. Along the way, a group of children runs after me. The sun feels hot and I'm thinking, *yes*, homemade lemonade stand. They're thinking, big kid on a big bike, *yes*, big spender.

"Hey, hey! Mister, mister!" they scream in unison. "MISTER! Come look at our stuff!" cries the leader of the pack waving a garage sale sign.

Sorry, Charlie, I already got too much stuff.

South of Toms River is Beachwood, New Jersey, which I'll remember as the place that broke my faith in Google Maps. I learn the hard way that Google's bike directions are not smart enough to know the difference between a plain old bicycle and a motorized, off-road wheelie like an ATV.

Turning onto Continental Avenue, I realize something is wrong. I'm out of road, but Google Maps isn't. The automated voice urges me on to Floral Avenue. I'm staring at nothing but timber. The map shows a network of streets, but all I see is an overgrown path into the woods. Just then, a woman in the last house on the road gets home.

"I see a lot of bicycle riders looking confused right where you're standing," she says, shaking her head.

I ask for directions to Floral Avenue.

"Those are paper streets," she explains. "They don't exist except on paper, and Beachwood is full of 'em."

Lesson learned, I proceed with caution. Google Maps scrambles to recalculate my route and goes haywire. Every 200 feet the voice orders me to turn left or turn right into absolutely nothing. To end this nonsense, I change the settings from biking to driving and enable the option to avoid highways so I don't end up merging onto the Garden State Parkway, which would be the cruelest miscalculation of all.

Finally I find what I'm looking for: the Barnegat Branch rail-to-trail. The former tracks of the Central Railroad of New Jersey, laid during the railroad boom after the Civil War, are now graded for leisure strollers and rollers. I pick up speed and enjoy a sense of progress for fifteen miles.

Helpful signs point out American holly, Virginia creeper, inkberry, white oak, red cedar, pitch pine, and poison ivy. At a clearing, I pause to watch kids cannonball off a trestle bridge and into a swimming hole. Their screams and splashes make me want to ditch this bike and join the fun. I don't watch for long. I need to get to Manahawkin where I expect an upgrade from last night's al fresco facilities. Instead of sleeping in the backyard of a host who is away, tonight I'm sleeping in a house with nobody home.

A few emails and one phone call confirmed my unusual plan. The father said his two adult children might be home for the weekend, but even if they weren't, he told me where to find the key.

A car is parked in the white pebbled driveway. I think I'm at the right house. The numbers above the door match the address in the email, but the reality of being here is just too weird. I stand next to my bike hoping someone inside sees me and opens up. Then I slowly walk to the front door, rehearsing for what comes next.

*Umm...Hi, sooo your dad said I could crash here for the night because I'm riding this bike and there's this website that he's on called Warm Showers and it sounds a little kinky but it's really not, it's like this Couchsurfing thing but for cyclists and—*the door swings open.

A guy in his early twenties is standing there with no shirt. His skin is bronzed and his pecs are chiseled and smooth. I forget my lines. He breaks my daze by extending his hand and welcoming me inside. Kevin works on an oil rig in the Gulf of Mexico for three weeks at a time. He's home for his week off but on his way out to meet some buddies. He says he won't be back until tomorrow night. Well, that sounds like an adventure. I think about asking to join him as he gives me the grand tour (and the green light) to use any bedroom or bathroom, and to eat whatever I want in the fridge.

America, is this normal? Because this is great. Why work a job you hate just to overpay rent in an overcrowded city? Now my mission is clear: I will travel the United States taking warm showers and cold food from homes across the Lower 48.

The doorbell rings. I'm guessing Kevin's posse is here, but he's still showing me around without shoes and a shirt. Dave and his girlfriend walk in. They aren't friends of Kevin's— they're friends of mine. They're spending the weekend nearby on Long Beach Island and want to take me out for an early dinner, which saves me from raiding the family fridge later on.

Dave smiles and holds six-packs of good beer in each hand. We head to the backyard and sit around the fire pit next to a man-made lake. I've never been to the Jersey Shore nor watched the MTV series, but I've always imagined that summer weekends by the water were for friends and family, barbecue and beer.

On my first trip down the Shore, I'm going to see it all but experience nothing. I'm not relaxing on the beach with pals and Buds—people or bottles. I'm alone on a gorilla of a bicycle eating granola bars and getting fooled by paper streets.

This moment is different. It's my chance to have a real Jersey Shore experience. I'm off the bike and with old friends and a new acquaintance. The sun is going down and we're by the water. It's a small lake with rocks instead of a beach with sand, but whatever. This sense of camaraderie is what I crave. Guys, please hang out here tonight.

David Joshua Ford could pass for a model even in a city with beautiful people like New York. He stands six foot four with wavy blond hair and deep-set blue eyes. If that doesn't hook you, his Australian accent will. He owns a small video production agency. We met last summer at a networking event. I recognized his talent and paid him to photograph me on a Citi Bike a month before I took off. I planned to use these "before" images on a website about my travels.

Dave's half-day rate was half a week's salary, so I wanted to cram in as much as possible. If this bike thing failed, I'd need a job. A new headshot for my LinkedIn profile might help. I showed up in a suit for photos around Madison Square Park and the Flatiron Building. Then I changed in his office nearby and carried a bag with assorted shirts to make the next series seem like it was taken on different days. First we rode to Times Square for a time-lapse sequence. Then we biked downtown and across the Brooklyn Bridge for skyline pics on the promenade and the waterfront below. I changed into a Brooklyn hoodie for photos with warehouses in DUMBO and street art in Williamsburg before calling it a (half) day over a burger and beer in a retro railcar. I have no experience biking across state lines, but I can plan an efficient itinerary.

After some beers by the lake, Dave takes out his camera. It's time for another photo shoot. He tells me to walk the bike onto the wooden dock and sit down. My feet disappear into the water. Something's not right. The bike doesn't look good, he says. He and his girlfriend tell me to peel off the blue painter's tape covering the logos. I resist but then relent. Anxiety is fading. Come what may, I've made it two days on a Citi Bike.

I wake up alone inside my private lake house. It's a big day. I'm headed to Atlantic City. It requires going forty-seven miles, the most so far. Google Maps adds bonus mileage by leading me around the lake to a paper street. I double back to find a better route.

Along the way to AC, I enter a corner of Wharton State Forest, the largest tract of land in the state park system. I don't have time to hike or canoe, but it doesn't matter. The road through the woods is so peaceful that all I hear are the spinning spokes. I marvel at the wingspan of a bird taking flight from its nest. No cars, just a big bird and blue bike in the wilderness. At peace, I ride on the double yellow line.

Nature's gentle rhythms turn into splitting headaches approaching Atlantic City. Cars return to the road. Lots of them, all going too fast. The shoulder pavement is broken and littered with wheel-popping debris. I'm sweating out the stress. Conditions worsen in West Atlantic City, which is surely not part of any state tourism campaign. Half-demolished hotels and bachelorette headquarters with plywood windows line the road, which is partially flooded.

Call me boring, but pole dancers and casino floors are not my idea of a good time. I'm an introvert and not a risk taker. I've never been to Atlantic City and never wanted to go. Yet, entering the city limits for the first time is a proud moment. I gambled and won, but not in any casino. I created a plan of action, followed through, and stayed the course despite an avalanche of doubt. I'm now more than one hundred miles south of my old office in Times Square. I am actually doing it. I am bike commuting full time.

CHAPTER 4

CAPE OF CORNUCOPIA

The stakes get even higher leaving Atlantic City. I am within striking distance of Cape May, the end of the Jersey Shore. I wake up on the second floor of El Dorado Motor Inn. My room is above a shop called Cash For Gold. Even the chain motels were too expensive, so for seventy dollars cash I slept here in the shadow of the Tropicana casino.

The bike fights me going down the outdoor stairs, the front wheel knocking into every metal bar on the railing. The beach is just a block away, so I pedal south along the famous boardwalk. The wooden planks remind me of the bikeway across the Brooklyn Bridge. Exposed nail heads make this an anxious ride, so I keep my eyes down, which isn't a bad thing. My takeaway from AC is that people need bigger bathing suits here in the Eden of the overweight.

Twenty miles from Cape May, my prize seems impossible. The road toward Sea Isle City curves uphill out of sight. My body begins shutting down in defeat. Then around the bend appears a "Peaches Are Here" signboard. Peaches? PEACHES!

Juice runs down my chin. Pulp clings to my beard. I devour the fruit with the passion of a zombie eating flesh. The teenage girl working the farm stand watches in horror. I approach with two pits in one hand and a few quarters in the other. I give her both and leave without saying a word.

When biking to work, I often dreamed of breaking free and riding a Citi Bike beyond the city. I'd fantasize while cresting the Manhattan Bridge listening to a German nu-disco song that I didn't understand, but the beat made my skin tingle in the best way. *Nie Vergessen* (Never Forget) became my mental escape anthem, ear candy that made life a little sweeter for four minutes.

Riding over the bridge into West Cape May, I press play. After so many times of my mind wandering atop the Manhattan Bridge, I've made a physical escape to South Jersey. I just Citi Biked down the Jersey Shore. The whole fucking thing.

I am happy to reach the end and even more excited to have some company. Unlike the first two nights, this time I am staying with a host who is actually home. Carol welcomes me inside with a tall glass of ice water, which I irresponsibly drink in two gulps. I shake the cubes, and she pours more.

Carol is a social worker and crisis counselor in an underserved school district. She has a soft face topped with short gray hair—a maternal look you trust instantly. Carol leads me upstairs to my room. It's right out of a B&B magazine with an antique metal bed frame and patterned quilt. A vinyl wall decal quotes Ralph Waldo Emerson: "Live in the sunshine, swim the sea, drink the wild air."

As we walk around the house, I notice yoga blocks and hand drums in every corner. Her husband Mark is a yogi drummer and is out buying beer; their son Christian will be home after his shift at the restaurant.

The tour ends in the vegetable garden, which is a maze of wooden planters. All kinds of goodies are growing out here. Carol shows off her zucchini, carrots, cukes, summer squash, and lima beans. The tomato plants top six feet. I'm surprised at the size and variety of their garden.

Carol responds, "Well, you know, New Jersey is called the Garden State."

Then it hits me. I've seen the puke yellow license plate thousands of times (and even uglier pale blue ones before that). I always assumed the state's nickname had something to do with flower beds in the fancy suburbs outside Manhattan. Having biked 165 miles down the coast, I now understand these gardens are about produce, not peonies. Jersey tomatoes are a famous summer delight, but Carol says sod is New Jersey's primary agricultural product. I am learning the better side of a state I once mocked for chemical smells strong enough to peel paint off cars driving the turnpike through places like Kearny, Elizabeth, and Carteret. I'm glad to replace the image of smokestacks with the fertility of Cape May. Still, those ugly license plates aren't doing the state's reputation any favors.

In the kitchen, chunks of pink watermelon are bleeding onto the counter. I go back into fruit zombie mode, sinking my teeth into the flesh and slurping the juice, piece after piece. I can't get enough. Watermelon—light, sweet, and full of hydration—is my new best friend.

In walks Mark with Dogfish Head and Lagunitas. He is tall, tan, and athletically thin with a wide smile that wrinkles his cheeks. We all head to the front porch with our choice of bottles.

Before moving to Cape May in 1987, Carol says she lived in Lavallette, the same town where I slept outside the first night. She met Mark there while waitressing. They hit it off and took a romantic weekend trip to Cape May. The rest is history.

"We got drunk and were hungover and said, 'This would be a nice place to live,'" she recalls with a laugh. "And exactly a year later we moved down here."

I sense their strong chemistry and affection for each other.

I want to ask them for advice about relationships and love. But first I need to find a new place to call home, and Cape May is making a good impression.

"So, what in particular do you like about being here?" I ask.

Carol inhales through her nose, pondering a response. "The breeze. A different pace. This little corner of heaven," she says, pointing to the intersection on Broadway where familiar faces walk and drive by. "This is it."

Hershey, a golden retriever obsessed with tennis balls, also seems happy here. He trots over to Mark with playfulness in his eyes and a neon ball in his mouth. Mark describes himself as a "physical enabler." He's a yoga teacher, drummer, bicycle guide, and carpenter. At the height of his drum circle days, he led team-building exercises at corporate events, the same industry I just left. He speaks my language. We have a bond. He tells me about extravagant events during heady times when spending was no concern to Fortune 100 companies. I worked after 2008, post-crash, having to please clients with champagne taste and beer budgets.

Repressed anger bubbles to the surface. Those employers who used me like a cocktail napkin. Why did I waste the better part of four years trying to please people who couldn't be pleased? And why do these wounds still feel fresh? I take a swig of beer. I can't change the past, but if I put more miles in between me and Times Square, maybe I can finally let go.

Carol says it's time to eat, a feast in my honor. My plate is piled high with pasta and pesto, grilled shrimp with tails off, grilled corn with kernels blackened, and those legendary Jersey tomatoes.

I met Carol and Mark two hours ago, yet we are kicking back like old friends. Their warmth and generosity put me at ease. I'm alone on the road with only a bike, but there will be more great Americans to meet and give me comfort. The beer and conversation keep flowing, moving from event planning to bicycles. My hosts have done tours in Canada and Cape Cod but dream of more.

"Biking across the country is definitely on the bucket list, maybe on a tandem bike," Carol says. "Like you, Jeffrey, I haven't seen the interior of the country. It would be fun to see it up close."

After helping with the dishes, I sit with Carol in the kitchen eating more watermelon. Christian comes home from work and a gentle mother-son interaction ensues. I excuse myself to get ready for bed.

I'm about to turn off the light when I realize my phone charger is in the trailer on the screened back porch. The upstairs hallway is dark and quiet. I use the flashlight on my phone and curse at the wooden stairs for creaking under the weight of too much dinner.

I step onto the porch, which is glowing by candlelight. Christian is on the wicker couch shirtless and strumming a guitar with a friend at each side. He's tall and thin like his father. Dirty blond hair brushes his shoulders, kind of like if Jesus played acoustic.

I was planning to grab my charger and go, but his friends are curious about their nighttime visitor. I take a seat and open a can of PBR. Five minutes later, two guys appear from the darkness with more beer, followed by more friends and a thirty pack. So much for having just one drink. They pass around something that makes my brain tingle. Does this happen every Monday night?

Christian and his friends are in the restaurant and fishing industries and don't work on Mondays and Tuesdays. This is chefs' night off. The conversation goes from biking to fishing. I get lost in the lingo and go upstairs to rest. Fishing I am not, but tomorrow I am crossing the Delaware River by boat.

Part Two

FROM CITY TO COUNTRY

*"We had longer ways to go.
But no matter, the road is life."*
—JACK KEROUAC, ON THE ROAD

CHAPTER 5

DELAWARE AND THE DELMARVA

From an Adirondack chair on the ferry deck, I pop open my laptop. I need to write about a most excellent journey down the Jersey Shore. It's a breezy ninety minutes across state lines, no effort required. River dolphins surface port and starboard. The boat has a food court and two bars. Wi-Fi is strong. George Washington didn't have it this good crossing the Delaware.

But trouble is brewing. Storm clouds with dark bellies and cotton ball tops line up like soldiers on the horizon. Over the loudspeaker, passengers are urged to return to their vehicles and brace for a strong cold front. When the boat docks, the crew, now encased in yellow rain gear, orchestrates the exit of automobiles with glowing light sticks. Not long ago in sunny New Jersey, I swaggered with confidence as cars waited for my bicycle to board first. Now my stomach clenches as I wait and watch taillights disappear into the growing darkness.

A man in yellow trundles over to ask if I'm gonna be OK. I tell him I wish I had his rain gear. I wear a cheap windbreaker that this storm will quickly get inside. A waterproof dry bag in the front basket has my shoulder bag with a laptop and Wi-Fi hotspot. My iPhone hangs in a clear pouch on a lanyard around my neck. The trailer has its own rain cover, but it ripped on day one.

The cars are gone and now it's my turn. Welcome to Delaware. Jack A. Markell, governor. A large blue sign greets me in the parking lot. The drizzle accelerates into a downpour. It's only five miles to Michele's condo, but the rain turns the road into a river. Soaked to my underwear, I plod along without panic. Once you're wet, you're wet. Embrace it. I take off my shoes and socks and keep going.

Route 1 is a divided highway that runs north to the capital of Dover. On the grassy median, I'm ankle-deep in water, waiting for a pause in southbound traffic toward Rehoboth Beach. Rain stings my face. Hissing tires fling water. I move to the edge, leaning into the wind. Then, with the resolve of Washington, I charge across the wet battlefield in bare feet.

Dry towels greet me at Michele's condo. My Warm Showers host has retired after thirty years of military service, which included event coordination. Everywhere I go, event planners! She now invests in real estate while working on a dissertation about how public policy affects our health.

Michele, a vegetarian since age twelve, is now vegan. She says 40 percent of kids in Delaware are obese and that health is important to her and the governor, who also bicycles. She shows me a photo of him wearing a cycling jersey with the state seal that says, "Office of the Governor Jack Markell." On the back it reads, "If you don't know the most bike-friendly governor, you don't know Jack!"

She is seeing him tomorrow for a ribbon cutting on a new trail near the beach. Do I want to meet Jack? A brush with First State political fame is tempting, but the early start and extra miles are not.

Instead I get to know her friend Jay, who is over for dinner. They are both super cyclists planning a trip to NYC later this month. It will be Jay's first trip to the Big Apple. They'll bring their bikes aboard Amtrak and cycle the perimeter of Manhattan. To give them a head start, I brought two fold-up NYC bike maps, but they turned into paper mâché on the ride over.

Michele asks me about outdoor eating options so they can keep an eye on their bikes. I say there's sidewalk seating at some restaurants, but unless your bike is like $6,000, I wouldn't worry about keeping it outside for an hour. A U-lock and thick cable work fine.

"My bike was $11,500," Michele says flatly.

My eyeballs roll into my throat. I thought this Citi Bike was expensive. How on Earth could hers cost ten times that? It turns out Michele needed a customized bike after hip replacement surgery. Every bike off the shelf was too long.

"I saved and saved my money for a few years and paid cash for an $11,500 custom-built frame. In fact, it's probably worth more than my car now, a Prius I've run into the ground with 106,000 miles," she chuckles.

While most people think $11,000 is an absurd price for a bicycle, Michele's reasoning sounds good to me.

"It's what makes me happy," she says. "I can ride and ride and ride and not feel any pain because that bike is built to my body. People get off theirs and are stiff and they hurt, but not me. I'm just tired."

By focusing on what's important to her—mind and body wellness—Michele finds happiness through cycling. And with that, we dig into a sensible dessert of cantaloupe fresh from the garden.

I stop chewing when Jay says he's logged more than 100,000 miles. On a bike. In a state with three counties. Starting at age fifty-five. Twenty years later, Jay is still going strong. He and

Michele ride together because the other Sussex County cyclists can't keep up. I ask why he got on a bike later in life.

"I wanted to lose weight. I was 220 pounds when I started biking, and I've lost about seventy since," he says. "I enjoyed biking as a kid and now I feel like a kid again. It brings back memories."

Short blond-white hair covers only the sides of his head. After retiring at age sixty from his TV repair shop, he rode 4,500 miles from Virginia to Oregon along the TransAmerica Trail. I have a lot to learn from Jay. I ask him about his trip over lunch the next day. We're enjoying free samples in the tap room of Dogfish Head Brewery, which might be Delaware's best export. After beer-soaked bratwurst and beer-infused chowder, we part ways with a big hug. It's time to hit the road to Maryland.

Before I left NYC, I planned my first seven days on the road. The sixth day was a ninety-miler from Michele's house in Delaware to another host in Annapolis. I'd cross something called the Delmarva Peninsula, which on the map looks like a Dr. Seuss character's furry hand pointing south to Virginia Beach.

What the hell was I thinking? Ninety miles is a lot on a road bike and impossible on a Citi Bike towing a trailer. I need to break this day into two parts, but the pastoral Delmarva doesn't have any Warm Showers hosts. I leave voicemails with municipal offices in Bridgeville (pop. 2,048) and Greenwood (pop. 973) about camping in their parks. No one calls back.

I keep going. On Delaware Route 16 my only company is corn stalks, soybean fields, and chicken farms. At lunch, Jay told me that meat from KFC and Popeyes comes from birds cooped up here or in Arkansas. If these chickens were outside now, they'd be getting fried by this sun. The shady side of a red barn with white trim invites a rest. I look at Google Maps and find a state park campground not too far away in Maryland.

Trees filter sunlight into strange shadows on the road to the campground. The place is deserted. I stand outside the locked office wondering what to do when a ranger magically pulls up in a car. He directs me to Loop A where I have my choice of all sixty unoccupied sites. Usually I like having first pick, but I feel uneasy being alone in the woods at night. I can't remember the last time I went camping. Maybe Cub Scouts? I set up a tent, foam pad, and sleeping bag and mark my territory by hanging a souvenir license plate on the trailer. Starting tomorrow, this orange and blue tag that spells "New York" will be fixed to the front basket of Countri Bike. For now, I've made a temporary nest in the Delmarva. Time to fly away and find some food.

Without baggage or helmet, I roll to the town square of Denton, seat of Caroline County. Nobody seems to be home here either. The only sign of life is two ladies and a man sitting outside the bar Public House. They watch me take photos with the bike in front of the town hall. I go over to ask them about dinner. I have two options, they say. This place or a fancier one down the hill, which becomes uphill after eating. The choice is clear. Feeling lonely yet social, I tell my captive audience too much about what I'm doing.

"'On the lam' means you're running away from the authorities," says one woman using my own words against me.

"Well, I'm not running—I'm biking, and nobody is after me," I say to reassure them. Then I show a selfie I took in front of the town's big blue water tower. A quick-dry neck scarf covers my face up to my sunglasses. It's the same color as the water tower. We match. I also joke that I look like a terrorist because, clearly, I'm not. I'm just a city slicker struggling in this country heat.

"You *could* be a terrorist with that dark complexion," the man shoots back.

Actually, that's a suntan. I don't know if he's joking, but I drop the conversation and head inside to use the restroom before sitting at the bar.

"Soooo, you're the one who stole a bicycle from New York," says the man next to me. He wraps a protective arm around his underage son, also at the bar.

I haven't even seen a menu and these small town minds have me pegged as an outlaw. The bearded bartender comes over and puts down a cold one and the ticket. He picks up on my shocked expression.

"Oh, it's happy hour," Trevor says, as I continue staring at the bill for $2.43. "You're not in the city anymore. Our regular price beers are your happy hour price beers."

I'll drink to that. Other patrons trickle in. They've seen the oddity parked outside and got tipped off by the gossiping gate-keepers. The words "stolen bike" and "New York" float around the room, but I let suspicion run its course. After the purpose of my mission makes the rounds, it becomes a team effort to figure out my route to the infamous Bay Bridge to Annapolis.

"The 404 is brutal," someone says. "Wide shoulder, but big trucks."

"Don't route him onto 50—can't take bikes there," says another.

"The ride up 309 to 18 is nice, but it's a crowned road. You know that?"

They're talking over one another, throwing out numbers that are meaningless to me. Trevor takes out his laptop to consult Google Maps. Turns out he rides bikes, too. Sometimes big gestures are found in small places. Two days ago I had never heard of Denton. Now I'm befriending the town's bartender. He plans my route and serves a perfect ahi tuna panini to complete my night.

He also invites me to freshen up at his place in the morning after he heard that I was camping. I woke up alone in the woods without any bear or mosquito bites but felt dirty from the sticky humidity. My neck is sore from sleeping on a lump of laundry stuffed into a pillowcase but feels better after a hot shower. His wife comes home from a run and they both need to get ready for work. They send me off with a banana, peach, and gummy snacks for the road ahead, where I face a big problem.

---------- **CHAPTER 6** ----------

A BRIDGE TOO FAR

A s a former event planner, I know how to plan ahead. And I'm calling for a taxi. Now. The Chesapeake Bay Bridge is a dual span steel monster 186 feet high and more than four miles long. It upsets enough motorists that a taxi service will drive your car over the bridge for you. About ten bicyclists a month also use the taxi because biking is illegal and for good reason—there's no shoulder.

Instead of a suicide mission, I'll get a lift. I'm not an EFIer. That's slang for die-hards who must bike Every Fucking Inch come hell or high water, or in the case of this bridge—hell high over water. I'm not trying to set a Guinness World Record for bike share. My trip, my rules. So I'm gonna fill in the gaps however I want. Escape from New York by ferry to New Jersey? Brilliant. Another boat to cross the Delaware? Absolutely. Taxi across America's scariest bridge? Damn right.

Before I left NYC, I made sure they had a taxi big enough to fit my bike. I called yesterday to confirm. Now I'm calling to schedule the time of pickup.

"How quickly can you get to the bridge?" the dispatcher asks.

"The van is going to the shop this afternoon. No rides after 1:00 p.m."

It's ten thirty and I'm still at Trevor's apartment, now outside on the curb eating the gummy snacks. There's no way I can get to the bridge that quickly. I explain the situation and that I can't go faster than nine miles per hour.

"OK," the dispatcher says. "What if we pick you up at the Nike store at Queenstown Premium Outlets?"

That shaves off enough mileage to possibly work. Google Maps estimates my arrival at 12:49 p.m. I have to be strategic. Route 50 runs directly to the bridge but has multiple lanes of heavy traffic. Back roads are safer but take longer. Safety first! Every minute counts. If I don't get there in time, I'll have to hitchhike or camp in the parking lot. I won't get the same hospitality from mall security as I did from Trevor.

Even with time not on my side, I stop at the old railroad station in Ridgely, once known as the strawberry capital of the country. Nothing beats fresh fruit on a hot summer day, and I sure wish I had some berries right about now. Trevor's peach is getting too soft in my covered trailer. I should have eaten it first instead of those gummies.

The story of public transportation here follows the same sad script as the rest of the country. Ridgely boomed with four passenger and four freight trains in the early 1900s. Automobiles slowly starved passenger rail, which died in the late '40s. Buses promised to be the wave of the future, and then those stopped running because everyone had a car. Freight service hobbled along until 1976 when Conrail shut down the line. A few grassy blocks along the former tracks have been converted into a bike trail.

Today, Ridgely's tracks and trail are quiet. A ceremonial caboose sits orphaned outside the empty station. I take a photo of the blue bike in front of the red train. My ETA ticks closer to one o'clock. I need to get off these back roads. For the final two miles, I swallow hard and merge onto the shoulder of Route 50. Semis roar by with disapproval.

I reach the Nike store with nine minutes to spare, but relief doesn't last long. The taxi is nothing more than a burgundy minivan without hubcaps. The front passenger seat is taken. Even with the back seats down, my stuff barely fits. The wheels take up too much space. The bike goes on its side and I squeeze myself on top of it, putting my chest and arms over the frame like a final goodbye to a loved one in a hospital bed. The scary crossing is no big deal; I can hardly see out the window. Fifteen minutes and thirty-five dollars later, I'm dumped on the other side of the bridge in the parking lot of the Maryland Natural Resources Police. Another hour of biking gets me to a condo in Annapolis.

I'm dripping sweat onto the welcome mat. Deborah's teenage son is wearing headphones that could fit an astronaut. Luckily, Ben senses I'm here. A rescue golden retriever turned down by two families, Ben howls and is joined by Cooper, a female yellow lab. Together they make enough noise to get the kid to pause his video game and answer the door.

Later, his mother Deborah arrives from the federal courthouse where she works as a court reporter. We exchange introductions, and she neatly arranges snacks and bottled beer on the countertop. Deborah, whom I gather to be divorced, says a gentleman friend is joining us for dinner and will arrive shortly.

"I would call him a gentleman companion, but that sounds too old," she laughs while slicing Jersey tomatoes. "Although he *is* older."

Mel has trouble walking up the front stairs after recent back surgery, but greets me with a hearty hello. His frost white hair complements the nautical navy and white stripes of his shirt.

He looks a little like Ernest Hemingway without the beard. Deborah and Mel kiss lightly on the lips.

Although not a cyclist herself, Deb enjoys hosting them because it gives her a reason to cook a nice meal. Tonight we're having a recipe from McCormick: arctic char with brown sugar and Old Bay Seasoning, which like McCormick is a Chesapeake Bay original. I assumed arctic char was white like polar bears, ice, and everything else in Earth's freezer, but this looks and tastes like salmon, my favorite fish. Deb says char is less expensive, but we agree it tastes as good.

After a cheesecake dessert, Mel heads home and the son returns downstairs to his gaming throne. I linger in the kitchen to learn more about my host. Deborah went to court reporting school right out of high school, but didn't pass certification. Instead, she spent the next twenty years at the home improvement chain Hechinger before giving her original dream another go.

"You gotta find what it is that makes you happy because you don't want to spend life doing something that makes you frustrated," she says.

That's why I got out of the events business, I tell her. Running around in circles to please clients who couldn't be pleased. One shallow emergency after another.

"I wouldn't even call it event planning. It was more like event scrambling," I laugh. That's my canned joke as to why I quit what sounds like a fun career.

Deb smiles weakly. Her mind is elsewhere. Sensing pain in her life, I don't want to continue my "So, what makes you happy?" line of questioning. Just after she got home, an appraiser came to the condo. I stay silent, waiting for her to guide the conversation.

After a minute she speaks. "I just want to wake up and look

at the Rockies. But that probably won't happen until I retire, and then you get stricken with some awful disease, so..."

The sentence fades unfinished. Ben and Cooper are sprawled on the floor with none of these preoccupations. We get pets to make us happy and take our minds off the daily struggle.

"I just gotta keep my eyes on the prize," she continues with a sigh. "And in the meantime, at least there's wine."

She tosses back the last of the chardonnay and surrenders her glass to the dishwasher. The machine whirls to a start. Deborah wipes her hands on a dish towel and rests them on the sink, elbows out, staring into the dark living room. Is she imagining the Rockies?

I have my eyes on a different prize. The nation's capital is just a day away.

------ **CHAPTER 7** ------

DC AND C&O

The ride from Annapolis to DC leaves me wishing for another bike taxi. I waste an hour at Deborah's house previewing the safest route on Google Maps, which is determined to send me on the busiest roads. I settle for Maryland Route 450. Tree branches reach into the narrow shoulder that is littered with fallen limbs, forcing me into the lane of traffic with a 50 mph speed limit. Drivers accelerate around me to get back above fifty.

Google Maps doesn't chime any greeting, but when I see a Capital Bikeshare rack I know I've made it to the District of Columbia. I roll past Union Station, the Capitol, and onto the National Mall. I stop at the Lincoln Memorial overlooking the Reflecting Pool. Seeing the Washington Monument in late afternoon sunlight brings me to tears. One week after heading into the unknown, I'm in America's capital and feeling confident. I'm eager to explore a new set of landmarks on the same old bike I know from New York.

My oldest college friend is hosting me for the weekend in Rosslyn. Jeanette and I are going out for Bolivian food since we both share a love for South America. We met freshman year at tryouts to be Spanish language drill instructors, but got cut on the same day. We also both double majored in political science, but only Jeanette pursued it in the real world. She's an attorney for the Government Accountability Office. She writes reports and gets agencies like the Department of the Interior in trouble when they don't follow their own rules.

I have one more bridge to cross and I'll be in Virginia, my fifth state in eight days. Not bad for a Citi Biker. Shadows darken the grounds of Arlington National Cemetery, making the white grave markers appear to float. My spine shivers. I walk the bike up a hill to see the Marine Corps War Memorial. I stop for a quick look at the Iwo Jima statue and cross paths with Mike and Christine, also on bikes.

"Well, well, you're a long way from home," Mike says, recognizing my brand of bike. They can't believe how I got here, but the evidence is right in front of them. We exchange Instagram handles and I pedal away, greeting Jeanette with a sweaty hug as the street lights turn on.

My arrival in Washington is timely. It's DC Beer Week and the perfect activity is tomorrow: Bikes & Brews, a ride sponsored by a shop called City Bikes. I can't wait to show Washingtonians my wheels while sampling their craft beer. I ride to Adams Morgan, a neighborhood I remember being sketchy in 1999 when I spent the summer living there for a government internship in college. Sixteen years ago was the last time I was in DC. With diverse restaurants and shops, Adams Morgan looks fine now. I arrive early and wait under a tree outside the shop. I don't know anyone, but other people want to know how a Citi Bike got to DC.

"Ah man, you gotta have a lotta heart to ride that thing," laughs a guy while snapping a photo.

A red bandana wraps his dreadlocks while a tank top exposes biceps as big as my thighs. He knows these bikes are sturdy. He used to live in NYC and tells me about finding a loose one on the Lower East Side. He and his friends took turns popping wheelies and riding over every rough surface they could find. They threw it down stairs. Into the river. Fished it out and bashed it some more. Despite the abuse, only the back fender fell off. The bike still worked, bruised but not broken. At least he left the bike in the city.

The group ride begins, and we make stops at Hellbender and Atlas breweries. I never have to wait long for someone to come over and strike up a conversation, such as an immigration policy analyst or young lawyers from the US Patent and Trademark Office. My best connection is with Saul, manager of the bike shop. He thinks what I'm doing is "rad" and offers me a free tune-up tomorrow. I quickly agree. I have no tools or pump and could at least use more air in the tires after 300 miles, especially before hitting a rocky trail out of town.

The next day I return with the Citi Bike, which is like bringing your own exotic animal into a pet store. Everyone wants a look at my species. Capital Bikeshare in DC is owned by the same company as Citi Bike in New York. The equipment is similar, but I'm riding the wave of the future. This model dropped a month ago and hasn't yet hit streets in DC.

Saul raises the bike on the repair stand and gets to work. He doesn't just grease the chain. He swaps out the couch cushion saddle and plastic pedals, one of which is already cracking. He says distance cyclists prefer clipless pedals, which I've never tried and would require $200 shoes. I can't. As a middle ground, I get pedals with toe cages to prevent my feet from slipping during climbs.

Everything is on the house. I can't thank Saul enough. His generosity gives me a needed boost of support. When I was having second thoughts going down the Jersey Shore, I told myself to hang in until DC where I'd reevaluate my ambitions.

Maybe DC would be far enough. After a weekend with new friends and old friends, I am energized to continue the journey.

The next week will be less social. I'll ride over rocks, camp in the woods, and pass through little towns that suburbanization skipped. I'm not sure how a Citi Bike handles off paved streets or how this city boy holds up alone in nature, but I'm about to find out.

Two ideals guide my planning: flat roads and no cars. That's asking for a lot in a country that nature built with mountain ranges and humans built for automobiles. Yet I want even more. I want scenery (hold the mountains), national parks, and historic sites. This fantasy comes true along a 335-mile path over rivers and through the woods from Washington, DC, to Pittsburgh, PA.

The towpath along the Chesapeake and Ohio Canal is a dirt trail that follows an old shipping route. The canal was an engineering miracle of its day, using aqueducts, lift locks, and tunnels to move coal, lumber, and grain. It was built during westward expansion in a race with the Baltimore & Ohio Railroad. The railroad was modern and the canal was traditional. Both broke ground on July 4, 1828, in a race to connect the East Coast with the Ohio River Valley.

Long story short, the railroad won. The canal was abandoned after a flood in 1924, but the towpath remains. It was almost destroyed during the automobile boom that made the nation hungry for highways. The National Park Service wanted to turn this dirt path into the Potomac Parkway to make it easy for cars to get to the campsites. In 1954, *The Washington Post* wrote an editorial supporting the idea. Congress approved but Supreme Court Justice William O. Douglas did not. Douglas hiked the canal every Sunday to keep his body and mind in shape.

Douglas wrote his own editorial against the plan. He called the C&O "a refuge, a place of retreat, a long stretch of quiet and peace at the capital's back door—a wilderness area where man can be alone with his thoughts, a sanctuary where he can commune with God and with nature, a place not yet marred by the roar of wheels and the sound of horns...Certain it is that he could never acquire that understanding [of nature] going sixty, or even twenty-five miles an hour." Douglas challenged the paper's editorial staff to hike the C&O's 184 miles with him. The media went along for the walk. Minds were changed. The parkway was stopped.

Today, the National Park Service manages this trail, but Mother Nature is the boss. The C&O will guide me up the Potomac River into western Maryland, climbing just 600 feet in 184 miles. That's a rise of three feet per mile. By comparison, the Manhattan Bridge goes up about one hundred feet in half a mile, a climb I did twice a day getting to and from work. The C&O will be easy street. It ends in a place called Cumberland where a new trail awaits—the 150-mile Great Allegheny Passage to Pittsburgh. In total, the two trails bless bikers with 335 miles of safe riding. No cars. No hills. No getting lost. Thanks, Justice Douglas! I'm ready for the peace and quiet he promised but unprepared for the one danger that could stop me. There are snakes and wild animals, but only one thing makes me more nervous—a flat tire.

I enter the path at mile zero in Georgetown, leaving behind pretty brick buildings where I can buy anything I need. A cyclist warns me with unsolicited advice: be prepared. The trail's jagged rocks have popped his tubes. I don't have spare parts because, well, I don't know how to use them. My dirty little secret is that I can ride a bike but cannot fix it, certainly not a Citi Bike with special parts. This could come back to haunt me when the nearest repair shop is sixty miles away and dear

Saul is even farther. I remember a painted sign hanging in my great aunt's kitchen. It said, "If it has testicles or tires it's gonna give you trouble." Life is a mix of risk and reward. With bike and trailer, onto the C&O I go with two testicles and four tires.

I pass cyclists, joggers, and dog walkers. A group of guys paddle board on the canal's still, dark water. These people have a warm bed and running water waiting for them tonight. I move upstream past a little stone house. It's quaint and symmetrical with two windows and two chimneys on either end. I learn this was company housing for canal keepers who worked day and night. Apparently the pay was so low that the house came with an acre of land to grow crops, which were traded with boatmen for supplies like coal.

At Lockhouse 22, I stop and read that President Grover Cleveland came here to clear his mind while fishing. That's what I'm doing without the bait and tackle. I wish that a lock-keeper's wife would open the little green door and greet me in an apron with a freshly baked pie. I don't have options for dinner or dessert and would gladly pay for some hot food. (The expense and weight of cooking gear were too much.)

With warm pie on my mind, I keep moving and cross a sandstone bridge from 1889 and the Catoctin Aqueduct from 1834. Canal life is gone, but this stuff is still here. I've traveled back in time, and life feels great without motors and electricity. My legs do the work as my mind and body wander freely in nature.

Now it's just me and the trees, no more people or houses. Butterflies dance as I ride. Other bugs do kamikaze dive-bombs, bouncing off my cheeks and forehead. By five o'clock the gnats are out in force, swarming aimlessly in place. It's August and even the insects are complaining about this thick humidity. My skin is coated with sweat, turning me into a human bug catcher. Black dots get trapped in my coarse arm hair and long eyelashes. I smash through spider webs, their sticky threads now on my head. I hope the webmasters weren't home when I destroyed theirs. Later, I almost crash trying to flick a Halloween-size spider off my shorts.

Just before dark I reach Turtle Run Campground, which has no turtles and no running water, only a hand pump for cold water. I'm a walking magnet of bug parts. A family of three sits around a fire. They look like professional campers with a tent as big as my Brooklyn apartment. I wonder what's inside a giant cooler next to a thirty-pack of bottled water. All this for two parents and their son. Do they need an extra dependent for the night? They invite me over and show me how to make grilled cheese in a skillet. Hot dogs and s'mores follow. This meal makes my day because the lockkeeper's wife never showed up and all I packed were apples, protein bars, and gummy bears.

Over the next week I chip away at my goal of Cumberland, Queen City of the Potomac River, and the end of the C&O. The trail hugs the Potomac whose lazy curves separate Maryland from West Virginia. Although the free campsites are on the Maryland side, sometimes I hop across to West Virginia to sleep on a mattress at B&Bs.

Church bells and freight trains echo off the hills around Harpers Ferry, a spine-tingling duet by faith and commerce. Both the railroad and canal used this river valley to push west. Harpers Ferry was a milestone where the B&O overtook the C&O for good. The railroad is still chugging along. Trains sound their horns and puff smoke as wheels scrape along tracks that disappear into a mountainside tunnel.

There's something magical about this setting where small-town charm turns one rest day into two. Even the geography is special. Harpers Ferry is where waters from the Potomac and Shenandoah Rivers come together and where the Appalachian Trail and C&O Canal Towpath cross on land.

Harpers Ferry is just a few streets on a narrow peninsula

between rivers. The place is so compact that the town hall, police department, post office, and liquor store all share the same building. Near the historic site I find a hostel room and, across the street, what has to be the largest soft-serve ice cream cone in West Virginia.

Once the day-trippers leave, the cobblestone streets are silent. The past feels present. This valley has a violent history. George Washington chose this site for our second national armory. It became a powder keg when abolitionist John Brown led a deadly raid on the armory in 1859. He hoped to incite a rebellion to free the slaves, but marines led by Colonel Robert E. Lee stopped him. Brown was captured and convicted of treason and murder. On the wagon ride to the gallows, he sat atop his coffin. He handed his guard a note that said, "I, John Brown, am now quite certain that the crimes of this guilty land will never be purged away but with blood."

The Civil War began eighteen months later. Some of the worst fighting was around here. I learned about this in high school textbooks, but forgot almost everything. Now I'm ready to learn again, in person.

I leave Harpers Ferry and take quiet roads to reach Antietam Battlefield. On September 17, 1862, the bloodiest day in American history saw 22,720 men killed, wounded, or missing in the "hottest of hornets' nests," as Union General John Gibbon put it.

On this afternoon about 150 years later, the Bloody Cornfield is baking in the sun. Sixty percent of one brigade went down here in thirty minutes, which is about how long it took me to find a shady hiding spot and secure my bike outside the visitor center. I'm just in time for a reenactment of Antietam cannons blasting once again. The artillery team's coordinated movements fascinate kids and adults alike.

At a street fair up the river in Williamsport, I check off

Maryland soft shell crab from my cross-country food bucket list. I squirt mango habanero sauce to give the fried crab two eyes and a smile, and take crunchy bites as I walk around. Outside The Smokin Toad BBQ, I come across three guys with touring bikes and small panniers. They're ready to hit the trail and ask if I want to join. I can't keep up on a heavier bike with heavier gear, but I say yes anyway.

We ride two by two. I'm in the back row with another guy whose name I already forgot. Low sunlight passes through the trees and onto the trail. The towpath here is a dirt road with grass in between two bare strips for wheels. Off to the right, the canal is a dry ditch. For the next hour I match their 11 mph pace. I've never gone this fast for this long. At least I don't think so. I don't have a way to measure speed, but they have Garmins on their handlebars. Honestly, I don't care how fast I'm going. I just don't want to fall behind and be alone again. This sense of belonging is temporary, but I'll fight with my feet to keep it going for as long as I can.

Suddenly, a loud thud. A branch catches the frame in the pedal zone. It's thick and white without bark. This could be the iceberg to my Titanic. The branch could snap the chain, and after I tumble over the handlebars, maybe my neck breaks too. But this bike has a chain guard and I have cat-like reflexes, kicking away danger without missing a stroke.

"Holy shit, dude, your bike's a beast!" yells the guy next to me.

With big tires and a rock-solid frame, Countri Bike is steamrolling anything in its way. I no longer feel the trailer behind me. For the first time, this bike isn't a burden; it's a blessing. It took a few hundred miles, but here on the C&O Canal the naysayers are proven wrong. A Citi Bike is an excellent way to explore America.

CHAPTER 8

THE PUSH FOR PITTSBURGH

"One eighty-four point five!" I scream while punching the air at mile marker 184.5, the end of the towpath. One thing has bothered me since the beginning, though. What the heck is a towpath?

I finally get the answer from a trailside sign. Boats in the canal didn't have motors because outboard motors didn't exist. To move, they had to get towed—by animals. Mules walking along the path towed cargo boats while speedier horses did the same for passenger boats. It took the builders twenty-two years to reach here, and they never went any farther. The race to Cumberland was over. The B&O Railroad beat the C&O Canal by eight years.

Church spires and red brick buildings stand out against the green hills and blue river. It's exactly what canal boatmen would have seen approaching the city. Cumberland is western Maryland's largest settlement and my first taste of civilization since I began the trail in Georgetown a week ago. I donate my old Citi Bike seat to a bike shop right on the C&O. They knew to expect me thanks to a heads up from Saul in DC. As I pump air into the tires, I also blow them kisses for not failing me.

I stop by the town's visitor center for a quick bite of early American history before dinner. Cumberland is an interesting place. Coal mining and glass manufacturing made this a boomtown. Breweries and boat building followed. America's first highway started here. The city became known for tire manufacturing. Before all this, George Washington used Fort Cumberland as a base to end the Whiskey Rebellion over production taxes. It's the only time a sitting US president has led armed troops. I celebrate his victory and mine with a brown sugar bourbon custard at Queen City Creamery.

I camp alone outside the YMCA for my last stand in Maryland and last night along the Potomac, whose soft curves gave me more satisfaction than the asphalt grid of Manhattan. My tent is a stone's throw from the river and even closer to railroad tracks that run along it. Apparently, freight trains don't sleep. In the dead of night, headlights beam into my tent and the horn jolts me into a woozy panic that I'm about to get run over.

Despite little sleep, the next morning I'm feeling good to start the Great Allegheny Passage (GAP) to Pennsylvania. Whereas the C&O was rocky and overgrown, the GAP is like a golf course. A tidy path of crushed gravel and limestone will lead me to Pittsburgh in five days. There's one catch and it's a long one: a 23.5-mile hill up to the Eastern Continental Divide. I would detour for days to avoid something like this, but it's only a 1 percent incline. It had to be gentle enough for trains, so I'm hoping the same is true for a Citi Bike.

Having second thoughts, I get lunch before the hill gets to me. I pedal into Frostburg, a depressed little city whose architecture tells me this place was once something more. A big mining town in the early 1900s, Frostburg coal was so good that the US Navy and Cunard Line preferred it.

I'm deciding between Pizza Hut and Subway when down a side street I spot half a yellow bicycle sticking out of a building. Attached to the wheel is the sign for Shift, a farm-to-table eatery. In the window, bicycle wheels hang with colorful glass saucers in the spokes. Groovy. If Countri Bike ever fails, maybe I will turn its parts into art, or at least send the wheels here.

The name Shift has meaning beyond bike gears, says the owner Jes, who gives 10 percent off to those arriving on two wheels. Jes is petite with a dark bob and Bettie Page bangs. She buzzes with youthful energy and wears an everlasting smile. I sense something homey about this building, a former liquor store that now has the warmth of an artist's kitchen. Jes says Shift is about a change to fresh, organic food.

Life hasn't always been this healthy. Jes dropped out of college and got into booze. She admits that owning a bar at twenty-one was "a pretty wild experience." She then helped a friend open a place called Bar Monkey where she made the pizza.

"Later, I realized I didn't want to be in the bar scene anymore. I wanted to help people but felt like I was hurting them."

Jes went back to school to graduate and worked odd jobs before taking another leap.

"I knew I wanted to do a restaurant, and one with local ingredients in an open kitchen," she says. "There are so many great farms around here growing corn, tomatoes, and beans."

Shift is that dream come true. Most dishes have fewer than five ingredients. Bread and dessert are made from scratch by a full-time baker living in the apartment upstairs. On today's chalkboard is apple tart with whipped cream, cheesecake with strawberries, and fudge brownies with salted caramel.

A state university brings thousands of students and professors to town, but small batch and organic aren't buzzwords in Maryland's poorest county. Yet, the experiment is working.

"People are really touched by their experience here, and I think it boils down to the fact that our food is wholesome," Jes says, adding that Shift is hoping to end its first year making what she projected in her third. I bet old Josiah Frost would be proud to see such an enterprise in his town today.

Inspired by her story, I ask how she did it.

"I just kept trying to move forward and didn't think twice about going back no matter how scary it got," she says. "And it's still quite scary!"

Conversations like this make me want to keep going to meet more Americans who have found their way in smaller places so I can find mine too—somewhere out here and away from crowded cities on the coast.

Back on the trail, the hill is no problem. I don't stop except for a photo at the Mason-Dixon Line. Giant stone blocks spell out Mason & Dixon—one letter is carved into each cube. This marks my arrival into Pennsylvania, state number seven. I've definitely heard of "America's most famous boundary" but forgot what the fuss was about.

Two surveyors from England, Charles Mason and Jeremiah Dixon, were hired to end a land dispute between bad neighbors, the British families of Penn and Calvert. Pennsylvania and Maryland settlers had fought over the border for generations until this compromise was reached in 1767. Before the days of chain-link fences and barbed wire, small limestone markers were placed every mile. A sixty-six-foot chain was used more than 18,000 times to measure the line, which was surprisingly accurate even by modern standards. That kind of manual labor makes my uphill morning seem like a piece of cake.

Both families lost their land in the American Revolution, but this line was used again in another compromise. The Missouri Compromise of 1820 determined free and slave states. According to antebellum geography, I'm back in the north now.

Unlike Maryland, Pennsylvania was not a slave state. I'm on the right side of history, but I don't feel good about any of this. I don't want to go north or south. I'm trying to go west.

I summit the Eastern Continental Divide at mile 23.5. The hill is over. Tears of joy flow into the Gulf of Mexico rather than the Atlantic Ocean. Nine miles later I'm in Meyersdale, best known for a maple syrup festival each spring. About 2,000 people live in the Maple City, but I can't find anyone. Across from my hotel is a drive-thru bank with a horse and cart tied up, no driver in sight. There's also nobody home at Morguen Toole Company, which is where I'm trying to stay. The four-story brick building dates to the late 1800s. Over the years it has been a hardware store, furniture maker, house of worship, and morgue.

I call and leave a message. A lady calls back saying she has to drive over to check me in. Private rooms are beyond my budget and a twenty-five-dollar bed in the "anonymous bunk" gives me the creeps. But for a little more, I upgrade to a real bed in a communal room with the bathroom down the hall. I pay thirty dollars cash for one night. Nobody else checks in, not into my room or any other. I sleep so well I decide to stay another day to catch up on writing. There's nowhere else I have to be, so why not spend more time in Meyersdale? My only lazy day activity is feeding quarters to the local laundromat. The next morning, I can't find anyone to pay for the extra night. I leave a note and get my bike out of storage, locking the door behind me. Nobody ever calls to get my credit card number.

The GAP takes the guesswork out of route planning. I simply wake up, get on the bike, and ride. I have no errands to run, no calls to make, nothing to do. My only goal is getting from A to B, then B to C, and so on across America. I don't have to think about where I'm going. I just follow the trail and call it a night wherever the sun goes down. I eat what I want and where I can. There is no end to my lunch break. No work emails to answer. No networking events. No appointments to keep. I'm on my schedule. It's my time and it's my way. My deadline is darkness. Nobody tells me what to do. I'm in charge of myself and have never felt so free.

After a night in Ohiopyle, I tour the Fallingwater home that Frank Lloyd Wright designed. People complain it's in the middle of nowhere, but it's right on the way west for me. Today is my three-week *bikeversary*. I'm rolling under a canopy of maple trees with trunks as straight and smooth as pencils. This might be the most beautiful part of the trip so far. Then my pocket buzzes with a call from a blocked number. There's one bar on my phone. I haven't talked to anybody in days, so I pick up.

A reporter from the *New York Post* wants an interview. Now. I know the tabloid is anti-bicycle, printing anything that portrays city cyclists are scofflaws, their favorite SAT word to describe us. The only assurance the reporter gives me is that this story won't run in the crime section. I try to chat while riding, but the call drops a few times and the reporter gets impatient. She's on deadline. She makes me stop. While clinging to one bar, we talk for forty minutes. Later in the day, I get a voicemail asking for photos ASAP. I want to keep riding but have to pull over at mile marker ninety-one and tether my Wi-Fi hotspot to my laptop, which rests on the flat handlebars. I connect my phone to the computer and wait for images to be sent to New York at the speed of Meyersdale maple syrup.

Light is faint when a freight train wakes me at a campground in West Newton. This past week, CSX Transportation, the successor to the B&O Railroad, acted like an out-of-control alarm clock. Their trains blasted through the river valley often and all night. There's no hope of going back to sleep, so I check email and see a message from WCBS 880. The New York radio station read the story in the tabloid. The article "Ride On, Man!" is surprisingly favorable, almost heroic. The best part is that the online comments are disabled. I didn't even tell my parents about the *Post* to spare them from reading what internet trolls would say about their son.

After a three dollar a la carte shower, I do the radio interview shirtless while slathering sunscreen on my face with no mirror. Then I slap on some pit stick. That's the beauty of radio; nobody can see what you're doing.

Sunshine dissolves the morning mist as happy canoe people arrive for Saturday adventures on the Youghiogheny River. Today is my last day on the GAP and I have only thirty miles until Pittsburgh. It seems like three hundred. The date is August 29 and summer is serving up one last scorcher. My skin is slimy with melting sunscreen. I feel like I'm dragging twice the weight of yesterday. I'm rushing to make the end of a bike sharing event where I can meet local cyclists, and hopefully one who will let me sleep over.

A guy riding in the opposite direction cheers, "Yeah Citi Bike, yeah Countri Bike!" It's the first time I've been called my trail name. Did he read the *New York Post*?

Dehydrated and dusty, I arrive on Pittsburgh's South Side half an hour too late. I missed the event. I fall to the ground next to a Healthy Ride station, part of Pittsburgh's new bike sharing system. My suntanned legs are coated white with limestone powder. I need food, a bath, and a place to sleep. I'm in a new city and don't know anyone or what comes next.

Across the street, a guy walks out of the REI store and over to me. Rob's heard about my story. He leads me to Over The Bar Bicycle Cafe. I sit outside while he goes in and brings out three summer ales. Two for me and one for him. I like Rob. I make one disappear like water on sand.

Rob is tapping all over his phone to tell local bikers that I'm in town. He connects me to a staffer at BikePGH who is organizing Pittsburgh's biggest bike event, which happens to be tomorrow. I'm buzzed and responding to emails on my laptop while on the phone coordinating an interview with NBC 4 New York. Apparently it needs to happen in the next half hour. Thirty minutes? Can't I get a sandwich and sponge bath first? Unlike radio, TV news has cameras.

At the next table, several ladies giggle at this two-ring digital circus. The largest pug I've ever seen jumps on me, tongue first. I don't resist my role as a human salt lick—this is my only option for getting clean before the interview.

"Sorry, she's a big kisser," her owner says, yanking the dog back by her pink collar.

"That's OK, so am I!" I shoot back to a round of laughter.

Rob takes me to a quiet spot overlooking the Monongahela River. I thank him for his support. I set my laptop on a low wall. I kick off my shoes and sit on the ground with the bike and river behind me. Just before launching Skype, I pop an entire package of mints into my mouth for a sugar rush. The adventure in Pittsburgh is just beginning.

CHAPTER 9

STEEL CITY PEDALERS

I happened to arrive in DC the day before the Bikes & Brews tour. Now I happen to arrive in Pittsburgh the day before their biggest cycling event. I shouldn't say this as a former event planner, but sometimes the best plan is happenstance.

I haven't registered for PedalPGH but am told to just show up and ask for Scott. When I meet him, he tells me about his own cross-country adventure right out of college. The year was 1999. No smartphones or social media. He and his friends didn't have any money either. So strapped for cash, they stayed in a hotel just once because of a tornado. They ate peanut butter out of the jar and washed in rivers and lakes. Their body odor could be smelled across state lines.

Scott gives me a bike jersey and bib number to ride the course, which ranges from two to sixty-two miles. I choose a seven-miler along the waterfront so I can get back and meet people at the festival with free snacks and beer. As much as you want, even the beer. They are way too uptight to do that in NYC.

After the ride, I walk my bike—still coated in white trail dust—through the exhibitors. I pass a tent for Black Girls Do Bike and think to myself, well, I don't need to stop here. Monica

Garrison proves me wrong. She sees the Citi Bike and comes over wearing khaki shorts and a gray shirt with her group's name. Surprised at her interest, I give my elevator pitch. It isn't enough. Her eyes light up behind square glasses. Monica wants to know more about my journey, like why I left and why this bike.

"In order to achieve your dreams, you gotta take risks," she says as we smile for a selfie. The nice thing about biking is that it's an equalizer. I'm white and male and she's Black and female, yet we instantly find common ground on two wheels.

Now it's my turn to learn about her. Monica has lived in Pittsburgh all her life, but only began biking two years ago. She started a Facebook page called Black Girls Do Bike to find other riders.

"I saw very few women on bikes who looked like me," she says. "I was surprised because it's addictive once you do it. You get hooked."

What started as a question—"Do Black women bike?"—turned into an organization with forty-five chapters. Women and girls of any color and ability can participate. "However, we do discriminate against men to create that safe space for ladies," Monica tells me.

I'm not offended. I ask if the group is growing fast enough to support her financially.

"Oh no, I'm a desk jockey," she laughs, mentioning her day job at Verizon. "That makes cycling even more important. I spend eight hours behind a desk and then I can't wait to throw off these chains! Cycling is my release. Helps me clear my head and think things through."

I'm smiling and nodding. Bicycling makes us happier. We found the same truth despite coming from different backgrounds. I have no kids, but after Monica had her fourth she wanted to get back in shape. Running caused a lot of joint pain.

"Cycling was the next logical step to get some cardio and I fell in love with it. I bought a bike and spent an entire summer just riding and taking my kids along for rides. It was invigorating."

Even her parents picked it up. "They now have cycling dates. Never in my life have I seen them on a bike before!" she cries. Monica has a way of inspiring people, yet she's surprised at how fast her group has grown and the effect it's having.

"I get emails all the time saying thank you for creating this. People tell me they're cycling more than ever and buying bikes. They are taking action because of this group. They are making a change in their life."

The last of the beer is tapped and the festival is wrapping up. I hug Monica goodbye and head off to meet Kieran, who works for Pittsburgh's new bike sharing system. Kieran gave me a morale boost over email days earlier when I woke up on the GAP full of doubt. After insecurity dragged me down the Jersey Shore, I found friends and support in DC. But for the next eleven days I rode trails alone with mostly insects for company. Sometimes I'd think about how good friends in NYC hadn't even texted me since I left three weeks ago. I was getting lonely. Arriving in Pittsburgh without anyone to celebrate with would be a sad finish to the GAP. Solitude in the woods is one thing, but being alone in a new city sucks. That changed when Kieran emailed me:

I just found out about your journey today and I gotta say I think what you are doing is awesome. I have always dreamed of a cross-country trip much like the one you find yourself on and doing it all by bike share bike is a very impressive feat. Let me know if my office can help you out with anything from bike maintenance or a tour of the city, or at the very least buy you a beer.

The promise of a new friend and a free beer gave me purpose to pedal harder. Another tune-up wouldn't hurt either.

Kieran's warm brown eyes and floppy ears make him instantly agreeable. He's young and has a full brown beard. Originally from New Jersey, he's a loyal Yinzer now and is wearing a Steelers bike jersey to prove it. This city bleeds black and gold. The Steelers, Penguins, and Pirates play different sports in the same colors. This is the only city whose professional teams are so matchy-matchy. It's football season and even the buses shout Go Steelers! next to the route number.

We ride down a new bike lane on Penn Avenue, which Kieran helped plan. He just graduated from Pitt and wants to get into urban planning with an emphasis on placemaking. He's helping launch a new bike share system and is excited about living in an up-and-coming city with tech offices for Amazon, Google, and Uber.

Our destination is Point State Park, home to a geyser fountain on a triangle of land where three rivers meet. It's also the official end of the Great Allegheny Passage that I started in Cumberland almost a week ago. Mist falls on me like a cleansing spray. I've biked 335 miles from DC to Pittsburgh along America's most accessible recreational trail. All on a Citi Bike.

Kieran takes off to meet his girlfriend, so I cruise around the downtown business district. The workday is over and people are fanning out to go home. I'm waiting at a light to turn onto Penn Avenue when a city bus makes a jumbo turn and cuts into my lane. I hop off and drag the bike to the curb when something else comes at me—a young guy in gold-rimmed glasses and matching blond hair.

"Hey! You're the guy from New York City! I work for Bike Pittsburgh with Scott. Come get a drink with me...it's my birthday!"

Sort of confused, I follow Dan to a table where his girlfriend and their roommate are seated. Dan puts my drink on his tab despite my protest. Our server interrupts us both.

"Damn, who brought a Citi Bike all the way down here?" booms Cedric with a laugh.

Cedric is from Canarsie, Brooklyn and knows exactly what's parked on his patio. He used to work at the Waldorf-Astoria where at the ripe age of twenty-three he had "all the keys to all the rooms," including the presidential suite where every US president from Hoover to Obama has stayed.

I know that hotel well. For tours and events I loaded passengers on and off coach buses along Forty-Ninth Street in searing heat and endless gridlock. I also worked in their two-tiered grand ballroom. Cedric likes party planning too. He once threw a secret Super Bowl rager for thirty friends in a Waldorf Tower suite and no one found out. Now that's the kind of event planning I should have gotten into. He moved to Pittsburgh for the opportunity to buy into this bar, fulfilling his dream of being his own boss.

We finish drinks and bike to a grill in the Strip District, once home to heavyweights like Heinz, Westinghouse, and U.S. Steel. The downtown streets are dark and empty, which intensifies the bond I feel with Dan as we ride together to share steak and more conversation.

Dan is the kind of guy you like at first sight. He has a bright smile and eager blue eyes that flash like light bulbs. His energy for life far exceeds his wiry body. It's hard to imagine Dan lifeless, but it happened one night after last call. He was biking home with a helmet and lights, but none of that mattered to a driver blinded by booze.

Dan hit the pavement and went into a coma. He was hospitalized for months. The driver fled the scene, but his mother—on Mother's Day—turned her son into the police. He was a repeat DWI offender with a suspended license.

I take Dan's hand. His scarred forearm flexes as he returns my grip. I thank God for giving Dan the resilience to be with me here tonight. I hope this young man's selfless dedication to bike education will continue to help others.

Making friends in a big city is hard. Making friends in your thirties is even harder. With my social circle contracting in New York, I didn't know how to replace college friends I was losing to the suburbs for children or to other cities for new jobs. I didn't expect biking to be a way to meet new people so easily.

Pittsburgh's pedalers are a hospitable bunch, like a mechanic named Evan who gives me a free tune-up at bike sharing headquarters. Bike champions like Steevo, eleven-time winner of the Dirty Dozen race, who hosts me for two nights. Bike advocates like Dan who buys me drinks on his birthday. And bike entrepreneurs like Val who believe in me more than I do.

Val is the founder of a bike tour company. She fave-bombed my Insta feed and posted comments everywhere. That's one way to get my attention. Then she emailed to see if I needed a place to stay. That's an even better way. I was already in Pittsburgh staying with Steevo, but I took Val up on the offer. She lives in Squirrel Hill near the campuses of Pitt and Carnegie Mellon, but attended neither. Born in the Italian Alps, Valentina has a zesty European attitude, like an ever-bubbling bottle of San Pellegrino. Right from the handshake, I felt her energy and knew we were going to get along.

She and her husband Michael start cooking a pasta dinner with zucchini and tomatoes from their garden. I unpack on the pullout sofa. On the end table is a pitcher of water with lemon slices and mint leaves. On my pillow is a Styrofoam cube with inspirational words on each side.

Val already knows my story, maybe better than I do. She asks detailed questions about things I blogged weeks ago. Over dinner I ask about her past. Coming from a fine art background in Europe, how did she start bike tours in Steel City? After a round of cheers, she explains.

"When I was twenty-eight, I was living in Germany with everything I needed. I had a well-paying job, decent apartment, good friends, a good life. I worked for an art collector in Munich who owned more than 10,000 works in a private house and public museum. Yet I felt like I was on the wrong track and my life wasn't going anywhere," she says, shaking her curls in disgust.

She quit her job and subleased her apartment. Val dreamed of living in an English-speaking country, so she applied for a dance program in NYC and got a visa. Next came the dreaded apartment search. On Craigslist she found a place in the East Village and moved in that weekend. One of her roommates, Michael, would become her future husband.

When her visa expired, she returned to Germany. "I went back to my old job. I walked into the same trap, but I needed the money. I was going to limit myself working there until I could find a solution," she says. "Michael and I tried Berlin together for one year. I had another job with a bossy boss and it was horrible. I was at a dead end in Berlin. I was fed up with sitting in front of a stupid screen working on projects that weren't contributing to anything. I wanted to do something I cared about."

This frustration sounds familiar to thirty-three-year-old me in a windowless office by the Port Authority. Val got an idea "that came from above." She should move to Michael's hometown and start bike tours.

"I thought there is nothing to lose, so I flew from Berlin to DC. Packing up and shipping myself to the United States was the hardest thing I've ever done. I was leaving everything behind. I cried a lot."

Things got off to a bad start. Michael's car broke down on

the drive from DC to Pittsburgh. (They should have biked like me, I joke.) It got worse when they finally arrived at Michael's apartment. The building had burned down.

"A rabbit in another apartment hopped out of an open cage and onto a curtain, which fell down on a candle. This bunny ignited not only the house, but a new life chapter of mine! We were going to move permanently into that place," Val says, putting her hands on her head. "But I'm actually happy it burned down because, well, I never liked it!" she laughs.

To test her business idea, she organized an architecture bike tour of Pittsburgh's North Side. Turnout was strong, so she went all-in. Val researched city history, watched documentaries, and learned the fundamentals of starting a business.

"I have to say that the US is a great country to start things. It's less regulated and easier. I would not have done this in Germany."

Bike the Burgh is the first activity of its kind in this city. Launched in May, it's gaining momentum by late August when I arrive.

"Here I am super happy," Val says, beaming at me through her glasses. "I am more proud of Pittsburgh than some people who are born here. This is my new home."

Finding a new city to call home is why I'm on this journey.

Our forks stab at the last strands of pasta. I roll the foam cube on the table and it lands on "Freedom." Val made this from a piece of garbage as a joke. But it's coming with me to the Pacific Ocean as motivation to keep pedaling to meet more people. Along the way west many will come and go, and a few like Val will stay with me for life.

CHAPTER 10

WHEELING INTO OHIO WITH REGRET

L ife was good for six days in Pittsburgh. Getting there on the GAP and C&O was smooth and scenic. Before that, I spent time in DC with Jeanette, bike shop Saul, and friends-for-a-day on the brewery ride. Now it's time to move on from the comforts of camaraderie and bike trails. Today I plan a fifty-two-miler to someplace called Wellsburg in West Virginia. That's the longest ride so far and, well, I'm not sure I can make it. This is my first day on real roads in three weeks.

Real roads have hills and trucks, shattered bottles and rusty nails. Pittsburgh had hills, but in the city they didn't seem so bad with new friends like Val, Dan, Kieran, Monica, and Steevo. I climb out of the Allegheny Valley alone. The outskirts of the city have faded homes with overgrown lawns. Some front porches are missing stairs, yet everyone has a late model car or truck parked outside.

As I walk the bike up yet another hill, I imagine a forested trail all the way to California, just like there was from DC to Pittsburgh. Then anyone could bike cross-country and not have to deal with rolling over broken glass next to trucks that drive too close. My prayers are partially answered when I find a flat way into West Virginia. The Pennsylvania Railroad's Panhandle Division is now a car-free trail. This railroad used to link Pittsburgh with Cincinnati and St. Louis. The bike path only goes thirty miles, but at least I feel like I'm getting closer to two big cities where I can make new friends.

The trail strings together small towns like Oakdale where I stop at the diner, creatively called The Diner. Like a typical New Yorker with no trust, I always lock the bike and take my shoulder bag and laptop with me. But here I leave everything outside and unlocked. Bells jingle as I open the door. Locals stare at my pencil frame from behind their breakfast mountains of bacon, sausage, and home fries. I don't mind the looks because my nose is in paradise. The air is greasy and buttery and I feel warm and satisfied. The smell of breakfast at a small-town diner should be bottled and sold.

The next bit of attention catches me by surprise. The young female cashier, dirty blonde hair wrapped on top of her head, hands me fifty-five cents change for a chocolate shake. With a sparkle in her eye she says, "It's been wonderful seeing you today." The way she phrases it makes me stop and smile. I suddenly feel at home in a place where I'll only spend ten minutes of my life. Unless I ask her out on a date and stay to see where things go. Maybe have a kid or two. Get married at the Pittsburgh Botanic Garden right down the road. I imagine this while sipping thick chocolatey goodness through a straw, a sweet goodbye to Pennsylvania.

The sky is blue and the landscape is summer green. Tall grasses sway in the breeze on both sides of the trail. In there, a whole lotta crickets sound as happy as I feel after The Diner. Butterflies float by. Grasshoppers spring away from my wheels swishing through the hard-packed sand.

This morning started with hills and broken glass, but now I'm moving through nature on flat ground after the perfect chocolate shake. I enter West Virginia for the third and final time. The first two were easy; I crossed short bridges over the Potomac like at Harpers Ferry. Now I'm entering the mountainous Panhandle that wedges itself between Pennsylvania and Ohio like a middle finger pointed at Canada.

The trail ends and I'm back on asphalt. A road that starts like any other becomes my Mt. Everest. I stop walking and let the handlebars roll back onto my hips. I grab the water bottle and rattle the last bits of ice into my mouth. I can't swallow; my throat is that dry. I'm out of liquids and don't know when this hill will end. I walk higher and higher, curve after curve, waiting for the saying to be true: what goes up must come down. When it does, I exhale and ride the brake down to a busy road along the river.

Dark clouds hang over Ohio on the far bank. Here in West Virginia, I can't make sense of the industrial shapes. Rusty conveyor belts raised high off the ground. What do they carry? Flames shoot from tall, thin cylinders. What is that from? Smokestacks puff, puff, puff. What am I breathing? The air won't stop hissing. What is that sound? This is coal country. Gas carbon plants make furnace and foundry coke. It looks like a sci-fi set in 2080 after man has raped Mother Earth of her last ores.

Extra-wide pickup trucks buzz me on the shoulder. Coal mines may be dangerous, but so are these roads for my canary of a bicycle. I've almost made it to Wellsburg. I'm down to the last mile, but it's all uphill. I walk the bike up to my hotel, a manor that is part rustic hunting lodge and part cinder block dormitory. A Google review sums up the experience as "beautiful during the day, but extremely creepy at night." There's nowhere else to stay and nothing to eat here except ice cubes from the machine. I celebrate a fifty-two-mile day with a dinner of three peanut butter protein bars that Val gave me this morning.

The next day I ride down West Virginia's Panhandle to Wheeling. A rail-to-trail along the river is an easy start under blue skies. I learn about the city's history from signs along the way. With its position on the Ohio River and the National Road, Wheeling became a center of industry, innovation, and wealth that rivaled cities on the East Coast. Iron foundries, glassworks, and textile factories flourished here. So did cigars. Marsh Wheeling Stogies were the blue-collar smoke of choice. Up to three million were rolled per week. Waterworks were installed before New York City and Boston. Firefighters started in Wheeling just four years after professionals replaced volunteers in NYC. Perhaps the biggest sign of Wheeling's early success is a bridge. It's the most important pre-Civil War bridge in the country and the oldest suspension bridge in the world still open to cars. And bikes. I'm going to cross it after I find some lunch.

I couldn't stomach another protein bar so I skipped breakfast. Now I'm really hungry. I lock up outside Coleman's Fish Market, family-owned since 1914. The smell of fried fish hooks my nose, but the Wheeling Brewing Company across the street catches my eye. The eyes have it. I drag the trailer inside the restaurant and sit against the wall. My server Josh doesn't ask me what I want, but what I'm doing. He wishes he could do something similar, although his cross-country dreams will have to wait. His girlfriend is pregnant.

He tells me that Wheeling was once the wealthiest US city per capita, but has fallen on hard times. So I noticed. Majestic buildings downtown are abandoned and covered in grime. Windows are boarded up. Parking meters rust alone while parking lot junkies cluster together outside the 7-Eleven.

"Well, at least you have cigars," I say. I can't stand the smell of cigarettes, but I'd try a Marsh Wheeling if Josh's got one. After biking through coal country, what's a few more toxins in my lungs?

"Nope, those aren't made here anymore," he says with a sigh. "The factory moved out of state. Our tradition for 161 years, gone."

"We're on the way back up!" Chad cries. The owner just clomped in with full cycling gear from helmet to clip-in shoes. His locally sourced restaurant is the first of its kind in Wheeling. Good things are brewing here. Chad uses nearby producers of everything from cheese and hops to Fiestaware. I thought these colorful dishes were from Target and made in China, but they're actually famous plates from Newell, at the top of the Panhandle.

A nice hunk of blackened catfish with veggies comes on a turquoise dish. I order their Panhandle Pale Ale to celebrate the good West Virginia vibes at this microbrewery. Josh says that I should spend the night in Wheeling, or at least the afternoon boozing here, but it's already two o'clock and the campground in Belmont, Ohio, isn't getting any closer.

On my way out of town, I ride past West Virginia's Independence Hall and the Capitol Theatre, which opened in 1928 at the cost of one million dollars. Then I turn the corner and go back even further—to before the Civil War. The Wheeling Suspension Bridge is right in front of me, its stone stained dark by time. Built in 1849, it was the longest suspension bridge in the world. It linked Ohio to Virginia, which became West Virginia when northwestern counties broke off at the beginning of the Civil War.

West Virginia is west of Virginia. And Ohio is west of West

Virginia. I've had to go south and north—even east after making landfall in New Jersey—but now I'm finally heading in the right direction. It's the only direction from here on out. Painted on the bridge is a big white arrow to Ohio with the words "National Road WEST." There is no more doubt. I'm heading into the Midwest, a prelude to a deeper west that lies beyond.

Why west? Because I've already been east. I was born there. Grew up there. Went to college there, in the Northeast. When I expanded my horizons after graduating, I flew to the Far East to teach English in Japan.

West is a new direction that I hope will turn into a new beginning. West toward the sunset. West toward my dreams. This is the way we Americans have always gone. Westward expansion. Western migration. Westward ho!

"Go West, young man, and grow up with the country," said New York newspaper editor Horace Greeley, years after the Oregon Trail and California Gold Rush, which also went west. So did Lewis and Clark before them. So did the railroads after them. Even national tragedies like the Trail of Tears went west. Dust Bowl farmers uprooted themselves and moved west on Route 66. Decades later, roadtrippers drove the same way. You could drive east, but it doesn't carry the same weight. No great American trek went east. By force or by choice, the direction of our footsteps, wagon wheels, railroad tracks, and automobile tires has been west.

The Wheeling Suspension Bridge was known as the Gateway to the West. It's part of the National Road, a paved highway that was the first federally funded project. It's so old that Thomas Jefferson approved it. The road began in Cumberland, Maryland, where I changed from the C&O to the GAP. It too went west and reached Wheeling in 1818. Almost 200 years later so have I.

In the river below, vintage boats compete in a regatta as the water refracts sunlight like a crystal ball. The vibration of cars on the metal deck shakes me. The same bridge so many Americans crossed going west in simpler times. Now it's my turn. I feel a connection to the past as I head to my future, somewhere west of Wheeling.

I'm not here by accident. "The Road that Built the Nation" sounded like a charming way to follow the tradition of Conestoga wagons that also wobbled west with no gears and too much stuff. But instead of falling to dysentery or Indian arrows, I'll survive by the grace of chocolate milkshakes and Google Maps. Any nostalgia for traveling the pioneer route dies on the other side of the bridge. A horn blasts behind me. A pickup truck clears me out of the way to make an illegal left on red from the wrong lane. The truck screeches onto the interstate ramp toward Columbus. Welcome to Ohio, state number eight.

The National Road, now Route 40, was probably better in a wagon than on a bicycle. The shoulder is blocked by dented orange plastic barrels, a sign of ongoing construction that isn't going anywhere. The sidewalk is cracked and impassible. I can't even ride the white end line, which is pitted with rumble strips. I must bike on the road with potholes so deep they could date back to the Van Buren administration.

The worst feature of Route 40 is not surface conditions, but the hills leaving Appalachia. Climbing out of the Ohio River Valley, I face the Blaine Hill Viaduct that almost breaks me. Built in the early 1930s for automobiles, the concrete and steel viaduct replaced a little stone bridge built a century earlier for pioneers moving west. The cute bridge over Wheeling Creek is still down there, but closed to traffic. This hill continues more than a mile out of sight. I walk the bike on the edge of the pavement and step on a mix of cigarette butts and roadkill.

It begins to rain.

Hardship on a bike should be Ohio's state motto. The next day, Google Maps sends me onto a chunky gravel road in the middle of nowhere. I play along. My tires can handle the rocks, but it's really slow going. Up ahead is a green sign for Guernsey County, a small marker I'll never forget because as I cross into the county, a pair of torpedoes launches at me. Two Doberman pinschers charge hard, barking commands I can't understand.

Target locked. Incoming.

I stop moving. Then I stop breathing, watching them get closer. Five...four...three...two...A loud voice shouts from behind the trees. God, is that you?

The dogs' owner calls off the attack. The Dobermans, silent and disarmed, lead me back to their master. God wears overalls and flannel. I thank Him and ask directions to the nearest paved road where I'd rather dodge cars than dogs. He says it's five miles away. On these rocks, that will take another hour.

Two miles later and still fighting gravel, I come across a scene that should be an oil painting in a museum. Children in old-fashioned attire watch me from behind a low stone wall. Their faces are wholesome, smooth, and pale like buttermilk. They dress like mini adults yet look like little angels. I think they are Amish. Am I allowed to talk to them? Do they even speak English? Did they travel in wagons on the National Road?

I stop pedaling, hoping one will have the courage to speak to me first. They keep staring with their perfect little faces. I'm in mismatched athletic clothing, dripping with sweat, and haven't shaved in days. I must look like the stranger danger from whatever storybook Amish kids read to learn not to trust outsiders. I decide to break the ice. I ask them, well, if they're Amish. Heads nod but nobody speaks. Another minute goes by. I've had enough one-sided conversations with myself on the road, so I keep moving, feeling convinced I've just seen the most beautiful Americans—Amish children—angelic and rare.

But wait. There's more! At the main house, women in bonnets chat on a wraparound porch overlooking the forested hillside. Babies sit in their laps. Men ready the black carriages for a trip into Quaker City, population 500. There is banter among the genders and some horse play—literally. I strain my ears, but can't understand what they're saying. I stop again, hoping someone, like an adult this time, will talk to me. They don't. I later find out they speak a dialect of Old German. Pedaling a bike, I feel a kinship to them and their simple horse and buggy. They are holdovers from an earlier time, the days of the National Road. They don't require electricity or motors to survive. On this trip, neither do I. I am a time traveler on a bike.

I spend the night with a host in Cambridge who tells me about the Depression-era glassworks that made this city famous. He says the process required twenty to forty people to make one single glass, which was etched, acid washed, and polished by hand. After biking through eastern Ohio, I appreciate how good old-fashioned people power gets things done. It's not the most efficient way, but the result is always more meaningful.

CHAPTER 11

OHIO TO ERIE TRAIL

A Cincy Surprise

The hills and headaches of eastern Ohio disappear leaving Columbus as I take the Ohio to Erie Trail toward Cincinnati. This is worry-free cycling at its best. It's a bike trail, so no cars. It's flat, so no hills. It's paved, so no rocks. It's a straight line, so no getting lost. A cross-country bike commuter can't ask for anything more, except maybe a diner with a chocolate shake to break up these corn and soybean fields.

The scenery isn't exciting, but with perfect conditions I set a new daily high of almost fifty-five miles to Cedarville. This trail town is home to a Baptist university. Tonight's Warm Showers host is a professor of mechanical and biomedical engineering. His lovely wife cooks a pasta dinner and leads us in saying grace. This is awkward for me, the only Jew for miles. I'm happy to hold hands, tilt my head, and close my eyes, but if I don't cross myself after, will they think I'm a bad Christian? I don't want to fake it because I'm not sure which direction to swipe. It's fifty-fifty, but getting it wrong could ruin my dinner and theirs. (Later I find out I worried for nothing; Baptists don't cross themselves.)

Three of four children are home. Their seventh-grade son just got back from track practice. He goes into the living room to ice his knee with one hand and uses an iPad with the other. For homework, he says.

A daughter in high school comes into the kitchen and introduces her boyfriend who grew up in Cambodia where his parents were missionaries. He speaks fluent Khmer, which he says is his first language. The two go upstairs to write papers in English. The oldest daughter is a slender blonde named Ella. She's the only child eating at the table with her parents and me. Ella just landed her first nursing job, which gets a congratulatory cheer with my glass of sweet tea. The absent child is at a volleyball game an hour away. She won't be home until nine thirty, yet her coach is calling for practice at five thirty tomorrow morning, her mother says with disapproval. I can't imagine such an early start. I usually don't hit the road until ten thirty or eleven.

"You have a big, beautiful family," I say. "I have just one sister, three years younger. She lives in Boston."

"Four to six kids is pretty average around here," the wife says. "But we know a few families with ten or twelve children."

I stop chewing. "They can field an entire sports team!" I cry, mouth full of pasta. "No need to drive an hour to the game, just play in your backyard!"

After dinner, Ella shows me around outside. A single oak tree with welcoming branches presides over the backyard. Soft September sunlight strikes the cornstalks on their neighbor's farm. In the garage sits a wrecked charcoal grey Hyundai. The front bumper and headlights were sheared off in a crash, and the rear bumper was damaged by the junkyard forklift. Ella and her father are rebuilding the car for her new commute to Dayton. To prepare for tomorrow's paint day, Ella returns to sanding instead of taking dessert.

Her father also likes to build. He tells me about his side business in wooden bicycles. He's flying to Toronto to supervise the installation of a wooden frame for a collector of rare bicycles worth tens of thousands of dollars. That makes Michele's ten grand bike in Delaware seem like a Walmart cruiser.

The parents and I continue to chat over sweet tea when in rolls Spencer. He's not one of the family. He's another cyclist. On short notice he called to crash here and arrives just before dark. Spencer is a twenty-two-year-old barista from Olympia, Washington. He had quite a following at an indie coffee shop, but quit to ride down the West Coast. He's now moving east on a shoestring by camping on roadsides and bathing in waterways. His goal is Burlington or maybe Portland, Maine, to make a new beginning on a new coast.

I smell Spencer before I'm close enough to shake his hand. Thin, tanned arms extend from his baggy tank top. He pulls dirty blond hair behind his head and dives into the leftover pasta like a shipwrecked survivor at a buffet.

Spencer and I have a sleepover in the basement, which has its own bathroom, kitchen, and home entertainment area. I claim the couch while he bounces onto the air mattress. It's fun meeting another cross-country cyclist. We stay up late and eat bowl after bowl of cinnamon Life cereal, which our host mother intended for breakfast. We talk about how awesome it is to eat cereal at midnight, especially the sugary kind our own moms wouldn't allow. Then we talk about our travels. He says "dude" at least twice per sentence and gets stuck on the word once he learns that I'm riding a Citi Bike. He calls his girlfriend to tell her. He also needs to smooth their long-distance relationship that is getting longer by the day.

I want to do some writing but can't sit up on the couch. I went almost fifty-five miles today. I'm going another fifty tomorrow. Fortunately, they're all trail-paved to Cincinnati where my cousins are waiting with open arms.

On my way to Cincy, I stop at Fort Ancient, a National Historic Landmark. The Hopewell Indian culture built these dirt walls five to twenty feet high between 100 BC and 400 AD. Scholars think they were used for social gatherings and ceremonies, not forts, because even a non-scholar like me knows that multiple entrances don't make for a good defense. I'm not stopping to see Fort Ancient, but to meet Dawn. She's been following my journey ever since *Bicycling* magazine asked her to take pictures for an article. Although the photo shoot will be in Cincinnati, she lives close to the trail and brings her two young children to meet me.

Under a green canopy, I coast through a pre-storm swirl of leaves. With a bright smile and soft eyes, Dawn radiates genuine warmth, the kind that leaves a New Yorker impressed (yet suspicious) at how nice Midwesterners are. She urges me to keep moving before it rains and sends me off with homemade zucchini bread. I ride just out of sight and stop to devour the slice as the pitter-patter of rain hits the leaves.

Aside from a stormy rest day in Harpers Ferry, this is the only wet weather since getting drenched in Delaware. The trees protect me and my shoes don't even get wet. I exit the trail in Loveland just several miles from where my cousins live. I've never been here before. They always traveled to New York for Thanksgiving, but my family never went the other way. Why would New Yorkers ever want to visit Cincinnati?

The next six days in Cincy blow my mind. I've been wrong about flyover country. This is my favorite stop so far, beating even Pittsburgh, if only because I'm farther west and the memories here are more recent. My cousins Mark and Karen and their daughter Michelle embrace me the way family should. They take me out for sushi, my favorite food and a welcome change from my road diet of burgers and onion rings. They introduce me to Graeter's ice cream with heavenly chocolate chips. Finally, they shuttle me and the bike fifteen miles down-town whenever I need to go.

Downtown I explore a revitalized waterfront and bike across the Ohio River on a suspension bridge even grander than the one in Wheeling. It was also a prototype for the Brooklyn Bridge. I see a Reds game with Mark. So what if they're in last place? Today they beat the first-place Cardinals. The rest of the family joins us for Vietnamese food at Findlay Market, an old public market in an older German neighborhood called Over-the-Rhine. Cincinnati takes its heritage seriously: Oktoberfest Zinzinnati is the largest such celebration in the US.

Findlay Market and Rhinegeist Brewery anchor this up-and-coming neighborhood that was down-and-out after civil unrest in 2001. Around the market are shops and restaurants painted bright colors, but another block over I see boarded-up windows and shady-looking characters. I'd trade my $1,200 bike for some real estate here, but I'm already too late. A proposed streetcar has jacked up prices even for crack houses.

Not for sale is the William Howard Taft House, the boy-hood home of America's heaviest president who weighed 335 pounds while in the Oval Office. In some photos he looks like the Monopoly man. Taft was not only commander in chief but also the father of the modern-day Supreme Court. He's the only president to serve as the head of two branches of government. He also began the presidential tradition of throwing baseball season's first pitch. Later in that game, Taft unwittingly started another tradition when he stood up from his wooden seat to stretch and the crowd followed suit. It was the middle of the seventh inning. But what I admire most is despite his heft, he walked four miles to work when at the Supreme Court. I bet he would have liked bike sharing, too, I say to the National Park ranger who asked what kind of bike I parked outside.

While in Cincinnati, I'd like to meet their bike sharing group. My timing is once again perfect. Tomorrow is Cincy Red Bike's one-year anniversary. To celebrate, Taft's Brewing Company is rolling out a special bike share brew.

The Urban Basin Bicycle Club uses the occasion for their weekly ride starting in Fountain Square. We head to the Taft Museum of Art for a group photo before cruising deserted downtown streets to Taft's Ale House in Over-the-Rhine. My bike stands out like a blue thumb, which makes meeting people easier. There's fashionable Fabiola from Venezuela who bikes with her Chihuahua named Jack in the front basket. There's bearded Dan who's into bikes and hikes when not coordinating accounts at a design company. And there's Taft's Ale House in a former church built in 1850. It has nothing to do with the president, but so long as the beer is good, who cares? Their website warns, "To serve a shoddy brew is an act akin to treason." I arrive with high hopes.

The dark wood interior is beautifully refinished. A balcony level bar looks down on the congregation of beer swillers. Fabiola, Dan, and I head upstairs to drink from a different angle. It's almost 10:00 p.m. and the Red Bike staff are gone. Dan leaves to ride home and get ready for work tomorrow. I call Mark to pick me up. On the way out, the head brewer intercepts me to hand over a glass of golden Red Bike Beer. One for the long road ahead, he says, as our glasses clink.

CHAPTER 12

DETOURS ARE FOR CARS

I'm old enough to have used paper maps when I studied abroad in college. I'd fold a street plan of Prague into squares and peek at it from my front pocket to hide the fact that I didn't know where the hell I was going in this medieval city. I would rather walk in the wrong direction for a few blocks than to blow my cover that I wasn't from around there. I imagined pickpockets in the shadows of Staré Město preying on tourists who unfolded maps on the cobblestone streets of Old Town.

Nowadays, smartphones make everyone look local. You're probably texting. Nobody knows you're really looking at that GPS dot to find your way. When relying on paper, going the wrong way can lead to unexpected and fun discoveries, but on a bicycle I don't have time or energy for that. I need technology to lead me straight to California with the fewest hills possible.

Google Maps is my copilot. It's great for driving, walking, and public transportation, but directions by bicycle come with a warning: "Use caution. May involve errors or sections not suited for bicycling." In each state this haunts me in a new way. In New Jersey, Google led me to paper streets that didn't exist. In Columbus, Ohio, I went the wrong way down one-way streets.

Now in Lawrenceburg, Indiana (motto: "Never heard of it"), I'm riding through the town dump on an Authorized Access Only road into the power plant.

Options are few where the Ohio River licks Indiana soil. US Route 50, the only through-road in this southern part of the state, is one big strip mall where cars swarm the hives of fast food. I'm trying to find the bike trail that avoids Route 50, but when I do, I'm stopped by an orange sign and green fence. Construction on a bridge near the power plant has closed this bypass for the last five months. The sign says the trail reopens tomorrow, which doesn't help me today. I groan and ride back to Route 50, praying that the gravel trucks won't hit me with anything harder than pebbles falling off the top.

A bend in the river at Aurora gives me an out. I turn away from heavy traffic onto a two-lane road to follow the river. The scenic route is so quiet that even the towns have disappeared. A green road sign for French is all that's left of a community that once had streetcars leave every three hours to Aurora.

A smooth ride on a wide shoulder takes me nine miles into Rising Sun, now known for a riverboat casino and hotel called Rising Star. A woman in glasses jumps from the sidewalk into the street to stop me. Chandra saw my New York license plate and wants to know what I'm riding for.

I don't have a charity cause. I don't know what to say. "Uhh... I'm escaping my old job" is the first thing that comes to mind. Chan has more questions. She's a reporter for the *Rising Sun Recorder* and interviews me on her front porch. With a worn spiral notepad and pen, Chan jots down my story by hand, interrupting me to point out a black butterfly laying eggs on a fennel plant, just one of many pots on the porch.

She then leads me into the backyard to see chickens, honeybees, and monarch butterflies she's raising for release. I guess this is what they mean by small town journalism. I love it. Two butterflies are ready. I cup my hands around one so it won't fly away before Chan can show me the difference between genders. The butterfly treads heavily on my skin. It feels like a hairy spider and I'm bracing for a bite that won't come. My skin is crawling, and I shake my hand before she can show me the black dots on the male's wings. She then walks two blocks to the newspaper to file her story, and I go two blocks to the Ohio County Historical Society whose relics educate me about southern Indiana.

The museum is closing for the day, but the curator, whose ancestors helped found *Rising Sun,* lets me poke around. Among the exhibits are pieces of farm equipment and a famous racing boat called Hoosier Boy that went 60 mph in the early 1900s. I wish I had that kind of speed.

The curator explains that Rising Sun was named after the sunrise over Rabbit Hash, which is the Kentucky town across the river and not some tasty-sounding breakfast dish. Rising Sun was once a port for flatboats on the Ohio River going between Cincinnati and New Orleans during the development of the Western Territory. It was founded two years before Indiana became a state. Rising Sun is the seat of Ohio County. With barely 6,000 residents, Ohio County is Indiana's tiniest in area and population. It's always been a small fry. The curator tells me it was formed during a drought that exposed enough riverbed to have the minimum area to qualify for a county.

My crash pad for the night is right on the riverbank amid alfalfa fields. "It is not much, but it has a good futon and a warm shower," write my hosts, Jeff and Diane. They call it their tin can. The tiny cabin feels like it's about to tip over, and I worry my weight in the shower will send me crashing through the floorboards and rolling into the river. The couple is planning to demolish it next year and build a new one. There are no bedrooms, so I sleep alone on the futon as they are spending the night at their main home somewhere else.

I'm invited to fish or kayak in the river, but that sounds like too much work after a day of riding. Instead I sit on a lawn chair with fruit, cheese, and crackers and watch the flowing water until sunset.

The next day, a forty-eight-mile ride to Madison, Indiana, is about to get even longer. Detour signs point cars up a hill and out of sight. Easy for them, but not for me. "Oh, hell no," I shout as I weave between Road Closed barriers. I'm going to press my luck along the river where it's flat. Three miles later, construction equipment cuts me off.

OK, Jeffrey, here we go, I tell myself, ready to get through this because my day depends on it. I flick the kickstand and wear a tough guy half-smile. I continue on foot, signaling peaceful intentions. I'm not about to blitz steamrollers and big boy construction trucks on a bicycle. My helmet and neon vest somewhat match their work uniform, so I hope this is enough common ground to get what I want. The first worker I see points me to "the brains of the operation" who is wearing an Indiana Department of Transportation vest.

"What the hell are you doing over here?" he laughs, pointing to the New York license plate.

I don't want to give him my life story. I'm sure he's busy. I give him a ten-second summary and five-second appeal for onward passage. He raises his eyebrows and looks down at the fractured roadway calving into the river like an asphalt glacier.

"The river's been taking this here road for the last forty years," he says. "We always gotta keep repaving it, but next year they're hiring private contractors to do it."

My interpretation is that he's going through the motions

and it'll be someone else's problem soon enough. Looking at my equipment, he has one concern before giving me the green light. "There's not a baby in the back of that thing, is there?"

I run back to the bike and walk it at a Wall Street gait through the construction zone.

"Oh, you don't gotta rush," he calls out. "We're not working that hard." We both laugh. As he escorts me, I wave to the repaver people staring from their beeping machines.

"Public relations, guys, public relations!" the supervisor calls out. The workers break out in laughs and inside jokes.

Pleased with how that went, I get back on the bike and take off my helmet. It's not just flat land that I'm after. Another advantage is that I have no traffic behind me until the detour ends in Patriot, a town with a footnote in American history for being the birthplace of Dr. Elwood Mead, the engineer who "made the desert bloom." Mead served as a top dog on irrigation in the days of Hoover and Roosevelt and supervised the construction of Hoover Dam. Lake Mead near Las Vegas is named in his honor. Without him, Vegas would be a sandbox.

I continue along the Ohio River, which hangs onto Indiana like a necklace. Its water was the lifeblood for riverside communities like Madison, the brightest bead. My Warm Showers hosts have a beautiful home with a view of the Madison-Milford Bridge linking Indiana with Kentucky. I have the entire second floor to myself. The shower is hot and powerful and has a built-in bench. I sit down with comfort as another fifty miles wash away.

Madison was built to be Indiana's capital, but never served as such. Steamboat traffic and river trade created a class of wealthy merchants. Handsome brick buildings on Main Street have small shops and restaurants much as they would have 200 years ago. When railroads became the highways of the nineteenth century, investment in waterways dried up. The hills around Madison were too steep to lay tracks. The town "slipped into a century of slumber," notes a tourism brochure.

Madison's misfortune had a silver lining. Since nobody cared about it, nobody bothered to change it. Madison today is one of the Midwest's prettiest and best-preserved historic small towns. The allure of timeless charm is tempting, but I'm headed for the future. Onward I go.

CHAPTER 13

BOURBON, BATS, AND BETH

I don't know what I would do without her. I messaged eight hosts in Louisville and only Beth responded, luckily with a yes. She's meeting me on the Kentucky side of the Big Four Bridge. I thought this must have something to do with their NCAA basketball team being perennial Final Four favorites, but the bridge is named after the Cleveland, Cincinnati, Chicago, and St. Louis Railway Companies. The trains are gone and now people and bicycles go across the industrial metal frame over the Ohio River. The sun is shining and the sky is clear. It's a beautiful day to enter the Bluegrass State.

Now in Kentucky, it's a short ride to her clapboard house on Quincy Street that she rents with her boyfriend Forrest. It's ironic that Beth, a vegan, lives in Butchertown, home to the city's original stockyards and slaughterhouses, one of which still churns out animal parts. Her front door faces a concrete floodwall in the middle of the road. It was built to prevent the Ohio River from drowning Kentucky. Should water rise, Beth lives on the wrong side of the wall.

None of that matters tonight because her garlic bread hits the spot after a forty-eight-mile ride. We eat standing up in the kitchen because our conversation doesn't break to move to the table. I peer through the screen door into the backyard. Roaming the vegetable garden are four ducks of different sizes and shapes. Their names are Quackers, Fudgesticks, Josephine, and Jemima Puddle-Duck. They keep company with a boney cat she smuggled out of Mongolia when in the Peace Corps.

Beth loves animals, especially cats. Mongolians, however, are deeply superstitious and terrified of them. While in the Peace Corps, she adopted a kitten from missionaries and called her Luna. Beth was writing grant proposals to conduct snow leopard surveys, but the local wildlife team spent money on bottles of vodka and got drunk every night. There wasn't much to do, yet leaving would put Luna's future in peril, so Beth got the local vet drunk and had him falsify vaccination papers.

Airport authorities were happy to let a feline depart Ulaan-baatar, but wanted to make sure nothing was hidden in the pet carrier. When they opened it, Luna escaped. "The cat freaked out and ran around the airport. All the Mongolians parted like the Red Sea, diving out of the way to avoid her." She finally wrangled Luna into the cage and got her own row in the back of the plane.

On a layover in China, the cat got quarantined. When Beth went to check on her, Luna was wet. "I never knew cats could sweat. She was terrified. I couldn't stand to leave her there, so I played dumb and picked her up like she was my carry-on and I needed to board."

Chinese authorities stopped her. The cat had to spend four months in quarantine. Beth put up a fight knowing that Luna would scare herself to death if left behind. Amid their argument, a Mongolian man entered the office. He couldn't speak Chinese or English, but Beth translated his Mongolian into English well enough for the Chinese to understand. Quid pro quo, her cat is on its next life in Louisville.

About my age, Beth and Forrest met on Myspace from a shared interest in cycling. They went on to start a pedicab business together, taking tourists around Louisville hotels, restaurants, casinos, and strip clubs. The business had legs (and wheels), but Beth's bike was rear-ended, and it shook her up so much that she stopped riding for a few months. She tried to rent it, but trustworthy pedalers were hard to find.

"The first guy didn't know how to ride a bike. He expected me to teach him! The second person did a good job for an hour, but then left my pedicab in the middle of the street to go up to a hotel room and do coke with his passengers."

For their next venture, the couple tried trucking. I can't imagine five-foot Beth making left turns in a semi. This gig didn't work because they spent more time on the road apart than at home together.

Beth is now a professional stilt walker who dresses as an eight-foot Statue of Liberty, Santa Claus, or unicorn. She does kiddie birthdays or promo events next to things like the world's largest toilet.

Forrest is more grounded as a lighting technician for gas stations. Adulthood began at nineteen when he bought a one-way ticket to Montana to attend a Rainbow Gathering in a national forest. He stayed for a month and planned to walk home to Indiana. Instead, he got a ride on a hippie school bus that broke down. Forced to hitchhike for the first time, he found that four wheels were faster than two feet, and he began crisscrossing the country from Indiana to Iowa to Colorado to Key West to Seattle. It wasn't only by car. Sometimes he'd hop freight trains. I have many questions about this, starting with how do you hop onto a moving train?

"The rule of thumb," he explains, "is to count the lug nuts on the wheel. If you can't, it's goin' too fast."

"Thanks, I'll keep that in mind," I say. "But where on the train do you hide?"

"Not in a box car, never there," Forrest warns. "They're usually older and the door can close and lock from outside. They can also get dropped off in the middle of nowhere. The best ride is in the grainers," he explains, "or the caboose, which is electrified to help push the train up an incline." He once got caught in a caboose and was arrested for trespassing.

"Man, you've done it all," I say with admiration. Counting lug nuts on freight trains sounds like a fascinating way to see a behind-the-scenes America, but I'll stick to back roads on Countri Bike.

"I've traveled pretty much everywhere in the country," he continues. "I also went to Canada and had under-the-table landscaping jobs. I illegally immigrated up there. They called me 'ice back' as a joke. I have a rule. Don't keep your job for more than two years. Unless you're moving up very quickly, there's no reason to stick around."

Forrest and I have very different backgrounds, but this I understand 100 percent. The longest I've worked for anyone was two years. Over time I'd get in a rut and want a way out. Now charting a course on my own terms, I am inspired by those with generous hearts and creative ways like Beth and Forrest. They make life work for them. Their dream is to buy a farm in southern Indiana, which I already know is home to great people. These two will fit right in.

After a buttery pasta dinner, we go out for a drink at 21c Museum Hotel. Forrest wants me to try his favorite bourbon, which Kentuckians drink like tap water. I'm not sure why we're going to a boutique hotel and not a Butchertown watering hole where men pass out on pool tables. Besides, Beth and I don't even drink bourbon, but three glasses of Blanton's arrive anyway. The amber liquid goes down slowly but smoothly. Forrest sips faster. He loves this stuff, but a fancy place like this makes him uncomfortable. Beads dot his forehead and his underarms are stained; he's sweating like a Southern politician. I'm humbled when Forrest picks up the tab. I'm not expecting my hosts to take me out, much less to the most expensive bar in town. I'd be happy passing around a bottle in their backyard with four ducks and one lucky cat.

Over the next three days, the happy couple takes me on a Louisville highlight tour. Roadside smokehouses turn my fingernails orange. We walk off brisket and mac and cheese at landscaped cemeteries with graves for American presidents like Zachary Taylor and fast-food officers like Colonel Sanders. We stroll belle blocks with historic mansions in Old Louisville and hang out at funky night spots in NuLu. Being with Beth and Forrest more than makes up for not meeting anyone in the bicycle scene here.

On the day I depart, I squeeze in a tour of the Louisville Slugger factory. I want to honor rec league memories of playing left field and praying that nobody would hit one my way. Dropping fly balls on the B Team didn't stop me from following pro baseball with a passion. Childhood friends, like normal boys growing up in suburban NYC, sided with the Yankees or Mets. Not me. I wanted to be different, and the cool logo of a blue jay's profile was all it took to cement my loyalty to Canadian baseball. Boxed away in my parents' basement are thousands of sports cards worth less than their weight as recycled paper. They take up a lot of room, and I keep reminding my mom not to throw them out. Not yet. They might be worth something someday.

The tour is informative. I learn that major leaguers order

between 100 and 120 bats a year and that with today's technology one can be cut in just thirty seconds. The sawdust goes to a turkey farm in Indiana and to Churchill Downs, home of the Kentucky Derby here in Louisville. Defective bats, the tour guide says, are sent to the Chicago Cubs who are in year 107 of their World Series drought. Everybody laughs. (They will win it all, finally, next year.) I leave the factory with a foot-long bat. I have no use for it except that it was free and I don't ever throw out free souvenirs. Besides, it might come in handy for self-defense down the road. I'm anxious about my route to Brandenburg, Kentucky, home to Jailhouse Pizza inside an old prison on the Indiana border. That's gonna be a fun dinner if I ever make it out of Louisville.

I stop at a downtown bike shop to ask about my route toward Fort Knox. Beth said I'm going across the wrong side of the tracks and should limit my exposure. Bells jingle but the mechanic doesn't look up from his work. My unusual ride is outside, out of view, and I don't bring it up. I cut to the chase.

"What are my options going west?"

The mechanic grunts but offers no advice. Looking at Google Maps, I fire off a round of names.

"Camp Ground Road?"

"Sucks."

"Cane Run Road?"

"Sucks."

"Lower River Road?"

"Sucks."

"OK then. How about Route 31 West? Uhh...also seems to be called the Dixie Highway. How's that?"

"Oh yeah, we call that the Dixie Dieway. You're not gonna wanna bike that. The Indiana side has much less traffic. Stay out of Kentucky."

That's not what I want to hear. Part of me wants to bike

Kentucky to experience a new state, but a stronger part of me doesn't want to end up a statistic. I cross the Big Four Bridge back into Indiana.

It's a little after 1:00 p.m. I'm at a red light in New Albany. Looking around the intersection, I see a giant logo for New Albanian Brewery stenciled on the side of a brick building. I've only gone ten miles and am way behind schedule, but it's hot and I might be thirsty. I turn right on red. A slow roll past the open garage doors, just to see, but definitely not to stop, I tell myself.

Three hours later, I've had a Naughty Girl, Bob's Old 15-B, Ancient Rage, and a crab cake sandwich. The beers and company are fantastic. There's Sarah the server, who is playfully hazing me. Food manager Stacy is biting her pen over paperwork while asking me about my journey, shaking her head at numbers that don't add up and my stories that don't seem real either. The only other patron is Matt, manager for a hazmat response company who must have been the local quarterback and homecoming king. He's been listening to my stories too. On his way out he offers a place to sleep, but warns that with a wife and three kids it's a noisy house. Matt lives to the north, which is in the wrong direction.

Comedy night begins at seven, and I could stay for that and crash on the couch in the taproom. Stacy has another idea. She wants to give me a ride to the top of Corydon Pike, a narrow uphill road with no shoulder. What I need is the brewery's delivery van, but only a Jeep Wrangler and her Honda Accord are in the parking lot. We try the Honda. Rear seats fold down and the logistics puzzle begins. No matter how hard you try, a gorilla won't fit into a fish tank. I'm on my own two wheels from here on out.

There's no way I can reach Brandenburg before dark. So much for pizza inside the old jail. I look on Google Maps for somewhere closer, maybe Corydon itself. Zooming in, I see pins for Indiana's first state house, Big D's Smokin Butt, Point Blank Brewing, and the Kintner House Inn. That's Hoosier history, barbecue, beer, and a B&B within a two-block radius. Sorry Kentucky, hardly knew you.

Hospitality here began with Kintner's tavern when Corydon was the state capital before it moved to Indianapolis. The current Kintner House dates from 1873. I settle into their smallest room on the top floor. It has a sloped ceiling and double bed with a Lone Star pattern quilt. Two handmade glass lamps with white fringed lampshades sit on a mahogany chest circa 1800. Like every good B&B, my room has a creaky wooden floor with flimsy rugs. I hit up Big D's Smokin Butt for some meat. I had enough beer for lunch, so I skip the brewery and go back to my quaint quarters to watch the Blue Jays play the Yankees on TV.

You'd think I'd awake early the next morning hungry to make up lost ground. But no. I can't move. My muscles say this bed is cozy and this town is small, why not sleep in and catch up on writing? At breakfast I extend my stay another night. Dee, the grandmotherly innkeeper with painted eyebrows, lowers my rate to forty dollars.

Suddenly I don't have anywhere to be, except in a rocking chair on the front porch overlooking the intersection of Chestnut and Capitol. After lunch, I take a break from writing and get a haircut across the street. Then I slide into Butt Drugs around the corner. This pharmacy and soda fountain has been around since 1952. I have a root beer float at the counter and snicker at the "I Love Butt Drugs" merchandise. I buy two magnets for a future refrigerator. You've gotta get off the interstate and visit towns like Corydon to find this stuff. I get dinner at the brewery and cap off the evening with more rocking on the porch as I plan tomorrow's route to the Christmas capital of America.

CHAPTER 14

SANTA CLAUS, YOU SUCK

I t's the second day of fall on the calendar, but I'm sledding ahead to December 25. I'm biking fifty-five miles to Santa Claus, who I guess spends the off-season in Indiana. Today I notice the first hints of autumn. A few yellow and red leaves stand out like Christmas ornaments on green trees, reminding me that I need to pedal faster west to outpace old man winter coming in from the north.

For now, all is well. I'm in shorts and a T-shirt. Route 62 takes me almost all the way to Santa Claus. The road parallels I-64 so closely that I see big rigs from FedEx, Walmart, and CVS through the trees. I am thankful they're over there and I'm over here where the pavement is smooth and traffic is light. I curve and dip through Hoosier National Forest and climb hills with ease. Yesterday's rest really helped. I also cleaned and oiled the chain. The bike is gliding more smoothly than ever. I let out roller-coaster screams on mile-long downhills.

A photo of the sign "Welcome to Santa Claus" is a must for Instagram. I learn that the town was first called Santa Fe. When it applied for a post office it was denied because there was already a Santa Fe, Indiana. Legend has it that at a town meeting inside a church on Christmas Eve, the adults were picking a new name when the wind blew open the doors and sleigh bells sounded. Children cried out for Santa Claus and the town has been trapped in the Christmas spirit ever since. It's a year-round financial blessing. Santa Claus Land became the world's first themed amusement park, even before Disneyland.

I finish the photo just as a shirtless guy runs by with abs from a fitness video. He's probably in his mid-twenties. We exchange a "what's up" and I soon catch up to him. Turns out he's a cyclist, too. He asks where I'm staying and I tell him the scary truth. I don't know. There's less than an hour of daylight left.

"I guess I'll have to stealth camp somewhere," I say, trying to keep the conversation going. There's a pause. I hear his footsteps and he hears my spokes. Will our thoughts align?

"What time do you get going in the mornings?" he asks.

"No time in particular, anytime really," I say, being as general as possible.

"Well, I'd let you crash with me and my dad, but I gotta get up at three thirty to start deliveries."

"What on Earth are you guys delivering at that hour?" I ask. Surely it can wait until after he makes me breakfast.

"Lumber. We have a family business, but we're short drivers right now, so we have to step in."

Lumber Jack, as I'll refer to him, wishes me luck and runs toward Christmas Lake glimmering deep blue in the fading sunlight. I turn into a shopping center that pretty much has the only food in town: pizza, Subway sandwiches, and a grocery store. My fingers thump on the handlebars as I replay the exchange with Lumber Jack. So close. Now what?

I buy yogurt, grapes, and M&M's and sit outside the visitor's center. It has free Wi-Fi, an electrical socket, and a statue of Santa to keep me company as I recharge my phone and look at

Google Maps for a place to crash. Cars in the parking lot dwindle until there are none. It's dark now. I'm alone and at peace with my situation until a cop shines the patrol car's searchlight my way. I get the message. Reindeer and sleds OK, but hobos on bicycles, no parking. It's a fine night to sleep under the stars, but I've never stealth camped. Apparently all the younger cross-country cyclists do it. Spencer, the barista I met in Ohio, did it behind churches, in cornfields, and next to fast food dumpsters. It's a rite of passage and my trip wouldn't be complete without trying it.

Tonight's the night. I settle in between two trees behind Saint Nicholas Catholic Church but don't pitch a tent. I want to keep a low profile because I'm visible to nearby houses. After midnight, the chill gets real. I pull the sleeping bag over my head and curl into a fetal position. I drift in and out of consciousness.

Wild noises disturb me. I see flashing lights. The Santa Claus police flush me from my hiding spot. I abandon the bike and run as fast as I can as the car gives chase, chewing up grass in hot pursuit. My sneaker slips on the dew and I fall down. The car stops behind me, its emergency lights swirling across the darkness. The door swings open and Santa Claus, wearing a beret and ammo belt, steps out.

This anxiety dream wakes me up just after five. It's still dark. The grass is cold and wet. My neck and back ache. I slowly gather my things and retreat to familiar ground. Back at the visitor's center, I pop open my laptop. The staff arrive for work and one invites me to use their conference room. I politely decline and finish planning the route to Evansville, my last stop in Indiana.

Evansville is pancake flat and its sprawl runs like syrup. Once again I can't find a free host. I use the discount app Hotel Tonight to book a $160 room next to a casino. For Evansville and for me this is very expensive. But I'm not "wild camping" two nights in a row. I need shelter. The bed is heavenly and the bathroom is palatial. I hit the rainforest shower for a long splash while the front desk staff, curious about the bike, Google me and start reading my blog.

Days blend together and so do the places. I pass through Mount Vernon, Indiana, and then Mount Vernon, Illinois. I'm plodding along back roads that separate rectangular fields. I can see for miles. It's like pedaling across graph paper and about as exciting as algebra. I feel like a pencil point on an infinite grid. The landscape is underwhelming yet overpowering. Now I get why they call this flyover country. But here is the heart of the nation where hardworking folks grow crops to feed the urban elite. Where an overlooked America works and lives. Where life revolves around farms, family, and faith.

It's harvest season. Supersize equipment demolishes cornfields, creating clouds of dust and leaving behind no survivors, only broken ears with shattered kernels. Some call it ghost corn. My bike looks like a Lego piece next to John Deere combines and harvesters with tires the size of houses and drill bits that can dig to China.

Bits of coal fly off dump trucks leaving an underground thermal mine near Carmi where I'm lucky to find a Warm Showers host. A Citi Bike from Manhattan, the most crowded place in America, is riding Illinois roads without a house in sight. Empty fields are dotted with nodding donkey oil wells. I pedal under overcast skies as gas flares flicker like wild lanterns. This agro-industrial landscape is eerie, endless, and fantastic.

CHAPTER 15

KATY, LOVE AT
FIRST SIGHT

The Gateway Arch appears on the horizon like a doorless passage to the west. My heart beats faster. I've made it to Missouri. I've made it to the Mississippi River. I've made it to the starting line of the west.

I had no idea anything was inside the arch, but when I find out about an observation deck, I have to go up. Now 630 feet in the air, I look down at the river and the building tops in downtown St. Louis. I feel the hope and ambition of those early pioneers heading toward the sunset in covered wagons for a new life in a destination unknown. I'm on a bicycle with less baggage and better maps, yet similar uncertainty. DC, Pittsburgh, and Cincinnati were great, but somewhere out here, west of the mighty Mississippi, is my American dream.

Less of a dream and more of a nightmare is Huckleberry Finn Hostel. Author Mark Twain worked as a Mississippi riverboat pilot and created the character Huck Finn, the carefree and poor friend of Tom Sawyer. Huck used the river for transportation, but it symbolized freedom much as roads do for me.

Maybe I am a vagabond version of Huck Finn. From Amsterdam to Yangon, I've slept in budget hostels around the world. This one has welcomed travelers since 1975, and there's been some wear and tear. The floorboards in the shower room have a hole big enough to swallow my bar of soap. The toilet closet has a bare bulb and a mirror on a string. There is no hand soap or lock on the door. A tiny trash can in the corner is vomiting clumps of toilet paper.

But, hey, for fifteen dollars a night, I'll bring my own wet wipes. I got a reduced rate for being on a bicycle and appreciate the discount. I lock the bike to the metal bunk bed. I have all fifteen beds to myself. I sink into the mattress like a baseball in a glove and fall fast asleep.

You might think I'm crazy for staying here, but I'm exactly where I want to be. Huck Finn is in Soulard, St. Louis's oldest neighborhood with quaint brick homes, coffee shops, dive bars, and divine BBQ. It's all walkable. In the vaulted halls of Soulard Market, established in 1779, I browse apples, pumpkins, and homemade sauces. Then I see the Clydesdales and taste hops at the original Anheuser-Busch factory, founded in 1852. Somehow they know I'm thirsty and on a budget because the tour leader gives me an extra token for free beer.

Beer also flows during happy hour at Trailnet, an advocacy group for pedestrians and cyclists. I can't believe how much space they have for so few staff. At my last job I shared a stapler with three people working elbow-to-elbow in "The Grotto," a windowless back office. As a joke my coworker put a decal of an open window on the wall. Trailnet has real windows on every wall and a full kitchen with beer taps. Our office kitchen had a mini fridge with fruit flies.

Taylor, the education manager, asks if I'll be on the Katy. I don't know who he's talking about. He says it's a trail, not a person. He's been many times. I'm still clueless. Before setting out from New York two months ago, I didn't think past the Mississippi River; I never expected to see it. If somehow I reached the Midwest, I'd take Bike Route 66 from Chicago skyscrapers to Santa Monica sunshine. Itinerary done.

Chicago to the north was out of my way, but Route 66 also passes through St. Louis, so I plan to join it here. Taylor warns me not to. He says that Route 66 goes into the Ozarks, worse for cyclists than the Rocky Mountains. Taylor says not to worry. He picks up a blank piece of paper and shows me the Katy way.

The Katy Trail follows the former Missouri-Kansas-Texas Railroad, or MKT, better known as Katy. Taylor says that when the trains stopped in 1986, the state got the right-of-way and turned 240 miles of tracks into the nation's longest rail-to-trail. From memory he sketches a map of trail towns with notes of where to eat and sleep. He adds details like the telephone pole in Tebbetts that hangs a key to the hostel and the old tree turn-off to reach a winery with views from the bluffs in Rocheport.

Thanks to Taylor, I don't even need Google Maps. Katy is easy on the mind and the tires. A crushed rock surface is soft and flat with just a few dips at road crossings. Sugar maple trees and sumac shrubs are blushing red and orange as I blaze west listening to the play-by-play. My Toronto Blue Jays are in the playoffs for the first time since I was thirteen. I remember sneaking out of bed and going up to the attic where on a grainy color TV I watched Joe Carter smack the World Series winning home run. Twenty-two years later, I'm using the ESPN iPhone app in the middle of Missouri. If I pedal faster, I could even detour north to Kansas City and watch the Jays in person.

The trees are getting dressed for fall, but this week's temperatures are back to summer. I sleep along the trail at campgrounds and the state fairgrounds in Sedalia. I've got perfect weather on the perfect path. These six days on the Katy are so easy that California feels within reach. I even dream of riding back to New York from LA. I'm blissfully unaware that in the states ahead, long after the Blue Jays fall to the Royals, colder weather and icy headwinds will make biking and camping impossible. For now, I ride without worry through forests, wetlands, prairie, and American history.

The Katy overlaps with the Lewis and Clark expedition. I stop to read about how their Corps of Discovery navigated three boats upriver with cargo weighing the equivalent of ten Chevy Suburbans. In 1804, Lewis and Clark averaged fewer than twelve miles a day. Suddenly I don't feel so slow. I'm getting better mileage on a Citi Bike and with similarly heavy equipment. Maybe in 200 years I'll get my own signage along the trail. Then again, I don't have to navigate sunken logs and mast-piercing sycamore branches, hunt deer for food, negotiate with armed natives, or discover 300 new species of plants and animals. Heck, I can't even make a campfire or change a flat tire.

Lewis and Clark weren't the only explorers to trek through here. This is Daniel Boone country. Boone became a living legend fighting the British and Indians in Kentucky during the Revolutionary War. He opened a route over the Appalachian Mountains for Americans to settle Kentucky and turn into modern-day bad drivers, at least according to everyone I talked to in Indiana. Boone was all about American exploration and expansion. He was the father of settlements along the river, including Boonville, where I first fell in love with the Midwestern delicacy of fried pickles dipped in creamy ranch.

Boone is a founding father of Kentucky, but he and his clan uprooted in 1799 when the Spanish governor of the Louisiana Territory gave him a land grant in what is now Missouri, where he lived until age eighty-five. You can hike to his gravesite from the Katy Trail, but I don't have time to visit and he's dead anyway.

Instead, I get the scoop from the owner of a trailside deli

where I refill my water bottle and buy potato chips. He tells me that Boone was buried next to his wife, but officials later came to dig them up and transferred their bodies to Kentucky's capital. Legend has it the locals pointed out the wrong graves on purpose, and two slaves buried at the family monument were taken to Frankfort instead. Forensic tests later showed their skulls were similar to slaves of the day, a colorful detail of American history I never learned in any textbook.

The Missouri River has taken many twists and turns since the days of Daniel Boone and those grave robbers, but the landscape along the trail looks about the same, minus the Kickapoo Tribe settlements and the addition of Clif Bar wrappers.

With no cars, the trail is quiet. I roll through shadow towns, my term for places now a silent shade of their former self. Some shadows like Nona have only an abandoned grain elevator. Others have a few houses sprinkled along the trailside.

Peers looks like another shadow town. I'm going fast with the wind at my back, but squeeze the brakes. Something isn't right. Shiny cars surround a whitewashed general store decorated with patriotic bunting. A three-piece band jams on the porch. I have a quick decision to make—pedal ahead or turn toward the action. The beauty of biking is taking a curiosity detour I might have missed in a car.

This detour lasts an hour. These are no ordinary townies. The ladies have nice clothes, nice hair, and nice jewelry to match their nice SUVs. I am a dusty mess with embarrassing tan lines. The wives on the porch see me approach and call inside to their husbands—Jerry! Bob! Norm!—to get out here and take a look at this guy. He's from *New York* and riding the trail.

These well-heeled folks are important investors in the Katy Land Trust that preserves the character of land along the trail. I'm invited to lunch, no donation necessary. Apparently the best chef in St. Louis is hosting a private meal for the group. How fast can I pedal, they ask. Not fast enough. Range Rovers and Mercedes drive off the grass and out of sight. Band members pack into a sagging station wagon. The town is back to a shadow. Only William and I remain.

William Fields is a landscape photographer who prints on metal, giving the images gleaming depth. He tells me the history of this store, now an art gallery where he's displaying some work. The river once ran right up to the front porch, he says. But in 1914, the Army Corps of Engineers constructed a dam, and a front yard full of water turned to mud. The store lost function as a port, but it came back as a depot when train tracks were laid. After the trains stopped, hiker and biker traffic couldn't sustain it and the store closed again. The Trust purchased the vacant property and turned it into a gallery for local artists.

This detour is great, but I'm still fifty miles from the hostel in Tebbetts. I won't make it before dark. William lives in Hermann, only twenty-two miles away and in the same direction. I've never heard of it. Hermann wasn't on Taylor's map. William says there's a winery, brewery, bakery, chocolate shop, and plenty of cozy inns and little museums. I'm sold.

Crossing the river into Hermann, flourishes of Deutschland are everywhere from food and architecture to business names. Every B&B is a guest *haus*, which makes me feel welcome given my last name. I set up camp in the city park for fifteen dollars. For dinner I walk to Stone Hill Winery, which dates to 1847. This was one of the world's largest wineries and earned international awards. The good times dried up during Prohibition, but tradition restarted in the '60s.

I've had a great day so I'm going all out. I start with a flight of red wine—three full pours for just $2.50 a glass. I order kassler rippchen, a German-style smoked pork chop topped with maple bourbon sauce. Sauerkraut and potato salad come on the side. I don't have room, but devour a slice of German chocolate cake anyway.

At dinner I read brochures from the tourist office. What is a German village doing in Missouri? Hermann was founded in 1836 as a second Fatherland by The German Settlement Society of Philadelphia who worried that native traditions were being lost on the East Coast. This site along the Missouri River was chosen for its similarity to the Rhine. Confident of future success, Hermann's Market Street was planned ten feet wider than Market Street in Philly.

I consider spending an extra day here like I did in small-town Corydon, Indiana. I could catch up on writing and enjoy confections from the bake shoppe and homemade root beer at Tin Mill Brewery. I decide to push on, but only after a fried catfish lunch at Concert Hall and Barrel Tavern, the oldest continually operating pub west of the Mississippi.

Back on the trail, a Noah's Ark of wildlife comes out to greet me. There are orange-tailed squirrels, white-tailed deer, black snakes, magnificent herons, and scurrying beavers. They cross the trail here and there and everywhere. I feel like I'm on an animated children's show with happy forest creatures bouncing along as boy wonder makes his way through utopia on a magical blue bicycle.

I'm sailing along when a brown blob makes me hit the brakes. I skid to a stop to avoid crushing it. It's a turtle. His name is Sammy. He seems to have fallen asleep in a bad spot. I get off the bike to see what's up with the little guy. He's not moving but he's not dead, so that's good. I ask a few questions, but his eyes remain closed. I resettle Sammy off the trail and continue on, leaving hearts and rainbows in my wake.

After passing through Jefferson City and Boonville, the river runs north and the Katy Trail turns south. Missouri River views are replaced by prairie restoration on the Osage Plains.

The Osage Tribe once dominated the tallgrass prairies of western Missouri. American settlers, in addition to displacing them, also destroyed the ecosystem by turning the fertile prairie into farmland. Less than 1 percent of prairie remains, and I'm riding alongside some of it. The railroad's one-hundred-foot corridor actually helped preserve native vegetation on either side of the tracks. Fun-sounding plants like big bluestem, ashy sunflower, compass plant, and rattlesnake master are taking root. Although it looks kinda boring to my untrained eye, I'm passing through ecological excitement.

About 240 miles of perfect riding wraps up in Clinton, which is the end of the line at least for this bike trail. Oh Katy, I loved your every curve. At the trailhead I snap a picture of a sun-faded green MKT caboose. Taylor's map has the phone number for a community center where I could camp, but I'm treating myself to a real bed at a no-star motel. After a hot shower, I celebrate the rural Missouri way with three fillets of fried catfish.

CHAPTER 16

MISERY IN MISSOURI

Nostalgia for lady Katy starts soon after I leave Clinton. Instead of smooth trails, I'm bouncing over broken pavement. Instead of the shaded riverside, I'm baking in the blinding sun. Biking on divided highway Route 13 is no fun.

I tell myself to keep calm and Katy on. I've faced rough roads before, but today's shoulder is a scary mix of rusty nails, orphaned automobile parts, and armadillo carcasses. Not just one dead creature, but dozens. It's like there was a war and all of the armadillos lost. Some lie belly up, bloated by death. Others have been squished paper thin. I don't want to adopt a highway. I wanna adopt an armadillo.

Based on the roadkill, I'm not betting on thirteen being a lucky route. I get off the highway and onto SW 900 Road. I enter a sea of rolling hills, a nasty surprise after six days of flat riding. I'm getting a taste of the Ozarks, which I thought I had avoided by taking Taylor's advice and taking the Katy. These hills aren't high, but they go up and down and up and out of sight. Gravel roads slow me to a crawl. The sun is hot and there is no shade. I finish the last of my water.

The farms are Sunday quiet. I am the only thing moving

through pastureland except for the cows. They stop grazing as I get closer and then trip over one another running to the far end of the pen. Horses are more intelligent. They approach the fence with curious eyes and interest.

Of interest to me is that roads in rural Missouri seem to have run out of names and numbers and were assigned letters instead. There's H and O, K and Y. There's also HH and OO. E intersects with B. Double V diverges from double D. Is a coded message spelled out for me on the edge of the Ozarks? Are the double-letter roads wider than the single letters? I'm tired of all this gravel. Which ones are paved and which ones are not?

Had I taken a different route, I might have encountered KKK. Not a triple-letter road, but the Church of Israel in the hills around Schell City, says a woman I meet that night in El Dorado Springs.

Finding El Dorado forever eluded Spanish conquistadors and it nearly breaks me. After leaving Clinton, I don't pass any services along the way. Just small towns with smaller post offices and maybe a Baptist church or hand-painted "Abortion is Murder" sign. That's almost fifty miles without so much as a vending machine or another Democrat. That's not good news if you're a progressive New Yorker with only one bottle of water.

I continue along State Highway E. By the time I reach Roscoe, I am ready to drink out of the toilet. Roscoe's population barely breaks three digits. The little yellow post office, which stands alone with a flagpole in a dirt lot, is smaller than my studio apartment in Brooklyn. And like every other post office, it's not open on Sunday.

I move on to residential streets, looking for a shortcut to Route 82, hoping double digits will be better than double letters. I turn a corner and see a house with a commercial sign that looks out of place. Farm dogs race to me and I tighten up.

"Alice, stop that right now and come here!" yells an elderly woman. The largest dog pulls a U-turn. His name is Allis, like the tractor brand. The woman is Madeline. She inherited Allis from her son who loved the brand but passed away. The laundry is hanging out to dry in the sunshine. Madeline, in periwinkle pajamas, tosses handfuls of feed at the chickens and questions me about what I'm doing on a bicycle in these here parts.

Madeline's family used to have a feed store and gas stand until Mother Nature robbed them of both ten years ago. The tornado was supposed to hit the next town over, but struck here instead. Madeline hit the bedroom floor of her hundred-year-old house as the winds destroyed it while her son got pinned by a pickup truck in the equipment shed, which collapsed.

"Oh, it was terrible. Just terrible! The storm just flattened everything that there was," she recalls. Everything was wiped out except a rusty pole with a diamond-shaped DX gas sign that had caught my eye.

I am not sure if her son died in that tornado or another way, but I don't want to get too personal. I'm just looking for advice about the alphabet soup of roads, like where is the nearest paved one? Madeline offers to fix me a sandwich, but a tractor combine is lumbering our way and taking up the entire road. My instinct is to leave now and outpace it. I forget about my thirst and part ways suddenly.

"I wish you safe journeys and I hope you find your way," she calls out over the noise, I think referring to my path in life as well as the way to El Dorado.

Farther down the road, a dusty pickup truck waits to pull out of a driveway, but there's no traffic. The driver rests his arm on the open window, tapping his fingers on the door and watching me. I slow down to invite conversation and he takes the bait.

"All the way from New-Yawrk," he says with a drawl. Another man and a young girl share the front seats, staring at me. Long wooden planks hang out the back. Why do so many pickup trucks carry long wooden planks?

"Yes I am...upstate New York...farming country," I lie, hoping to rebrand myself from being a city slicker. "Say, do you know where the nearest store is? I'm dying out here. I've got nothing to drink."

"Well now, you got Susi Q's back the way you came. They got sandwiches in there. Turn right at the little store, about three miles back."

There's no way I'm backtracking to see if Susi Q is buttering buns on a Sunday.

"Otherwise you gotta take this Route 82 all the way to El Do-ray-dah, and that's another twelve, fifteen miles," he says.

I puff my cheeks like I'm holding in vomit. I'm sick of this. Take me to town, dammit, I demand silently. I'm done riding for the day and bet I can fit in the bed of the truck. But it turns toward El Dorado and motors out of sight. I spend the next few miles wondering if El Do-ray-dah is how they pronounce El Dorado, sounding out both versions until realizing that I just don't care. Empty Aquafina bottles and crushed soda cans tease me from the roadside.

I begin climbing uphill, wondering if this will be what kills me. Ahead, three children run across the road while their mother stands watch on the shoulder. She sees me coming and the New York license plate again breaks the ice.

"So did you really bike from New York?"

"Yes. Hi. Where is the nearest store?"

She chuckles at the apparent absurdity of the question. "Oh, there's not anything around here for miles."

I'm not amused. I'm on the verge of tears. I tell her I've been biking since Clinton and didn't expect it to be so hot and ran out of water. She calls to her husband to check out this biker guy from New York and bring a can of Coke. He's thirsty.

"Dah ya want a beer instead?" he hollers from across the fire. They're burning trash in their yard. I pass no judgment. I just close my eyes to feel sweet, sweet soda trickle down my throat. I want to ask for a beer to wash away the sugar, or maybe another soda, but the kids are back. I tuck the empty can into my trailer to prevent it from getting tossed into the fire. I will recycle it later.

Fueled by a can of Coke, I pedal another six miles into Eldo, but am flagging by the time I hit downtown, which consists of empty storefronts, a Mexican restaurant, and a hundred-year-old opera house movie theater, which is also empty. I consider stopping by the police station to ask about camping in the park, but I want running water and a television to watch playoff baseball. A local motel is a mile away.

I'm walking up my last hill when a man in a black Vietnam Veteran hat calls out to me. He's smoking a cigar on the porch of a clapboard and brick house. Jack invites me over for a cold bottle of water, which I quickly drain. Crushing the plastic, I am handed another while he sips a Bud Light.

"I majored in booze and women, and Vietnam thought that sounded good, so I was drafted and shipped outta here," he tells me.

As he talks about his past, I get lost in his comings and goings from California, metro Boston, and the Midwest. Jack has been all over the country for work, most recently as a head-hunter where he "made a fortune." He moved back here twenty years ago. His wife died of cancer, but his younger friend Robin keeps him company. After a cigarette, she goes back inside to watch the football game.

Jack knows what bike share is because his son rides a Miami Citi Bike to work as the bar manager of the Delano boutique hotel where he, too, "makes a fortune." Maybe I should change course for South Beach.

This is a moment I will cherish. Me and Jack. Shooting the breeze on a front porch in Anytown, USA. He confirms there is one motel near here, and while not up to the Delano's standards, it should do for a night. If I'm not satisfied, I'm welcome to come back and he'll put me up. I thank him for the offer and the water.

C&J Motel is my third in a row owned by an Indian family, which is interesting because they are the only brown faces I've seen since St. Louis. Susan isn't surprised. She's the owner of the car wash and is using the motel's public laundry. She jokes that this area is as diverse as vanilla icing. I explain my difficult day over gravel, hills, and confusing letters from Clinton through nothing to Roscoe, also nothing, to here.

"Well, at least you didn't come through Schell City," she says.

"Wait, why, what did I miss there?"

Susan smiles and softly repeats three letters that hit me like a gut punch.

"It's a good thing you're not..." she clicks her tongue, raises her eyebrows, and turns to the dryer. "There was an Indian owner of the mini mart down the street. They ran him right out of town."

"What about this motel guy? He's Indian!" I cry, suddenly worried for his safety and mine should torches come in the middle of the night.

"Maybe not yet. He's new," she says softly, shrugging her shoulders. "I don't mean to scare you. You're not going towards Schell City anyway."

And with that she takes clothes out of the dryer and walks out, leaving me alone with even more questions. KKK country. This is where I am now? I could only imagine such a place growing up in a substantially Jewish suburb of New York City, but here I am riding around the edge of extremism in western Missouri. I'm not Black, but I am Jewish, not obviously so, but if questioned how would I mask my identity? Recite passages from the New Testament? What if they think I'm gay? I wear form-fitting clothing and ride a bicycle, and that's pretty queer for around here.

Racism, anti-Semitism, and homophobia are abstract but real threats. The landscape ahead is about to shift and for the worse. It all begins on Route 66—known as the Mother Road—that I quickly learn is one old bitch.

Part Three

WINNING
THE WEST

"Every calamity is to be overcome by endurance."
—Virgil

CHAPTER 17

ROUTE 66, ADD ANOTHER 6

I hit the Mother Road with high expectations. Route 66 will show me the America I never knew. Growing up in New York, I had no idea where Route 66 started or ended. It was a cultural thing before my time, somewhere out there and not close to me by distance or decade. Now I get to see what the hype is about from whatever remains.

Bicycle Route 66 gives me confidence. It overlaps much of the real Route 66 for cars. An organization called Adventure Cycling makes these long-distance bike routes. I wake up in Joplin, southwest Missouri, halfway across America and feel like I've been through the harder half. I hope Bike Route 66 makes riding easier. No more wasted mornings previewing streets on Google Maps. I'll simply follow this legendary road to LA—bike lanes and sunshine straight to the Golden State.

Not so fast, sneers old Mother Road. Her skin is cracked. Her shoulders are missing. Her vitality is gone. Only learning about this road's history keeps me from lashing out at the people who thought it was safe for biking. Stopping at two Route 66 museums in Oklahoma, I learn to appreciate the development of something we take for granted—roads!—and how small towns thrived on traffic during the golden age of automobiles.

Long-distance roads have been a priority since the Jefferson administration when the National Road was chartered to link the Ohio River with the East Coast. I spent a difficult day on part of this road wheeling from West Virginia into Ohio over Appalachian hills. The National Road reached central Illinois before it made more sense to forge west with railroads, which were making better progress.

America's desire for roads didn't abate. In the 1870s, bicyclists started the Good Roads Movement to improve dirt roads. Automobilists and politicians then took up that campaign to move people and commerce faster. A federal act to build highways in 1921 matched state spending with federal dollars. This led to more roads, but they weren't organized across state lines.

Enter US 66. Commissioned in 1926, it fused eighteen older highways into one long stretch. After some confusion, I realize that Route 66 is not just one fixed route. Like a winding river changing course, the alignment shifted a block north or south. Businesses boomed or busted accordingly. What never changed was the start in Chicago's Grant Park and the finish at Santa Monica Pier. In between stretches some 2,448 miles that symbolize the gasoline-fueled dream of the Great American Road Trip. The same road trip I'm taking without the car or gas.

A bike gives me the same freedom and more satisfaction. Don't take my word for it. Susan B. Anthony said that bikes did more to emancipate women than anything else, and that's coming from the mother of the women's rights movement. Anthony, a suffragist, didn't live long enough to cast a ballot or see the Mother Road built. But is there any other road with more songs and stories? America's Main Street is America's Highway and the Will Rogers Highway. It inspired Bobby Troup's song "Get Your Kicks on Route 66" that Nat King Cole made into a hit. In *The Grapes of Wrath*, John Steinbeck wrote about Depression-era Dust Bowl farmers who hit "the road of flight" to California in search of better opportunities. He called it the Mother Road.

I stare at the museum's black and white photos of these families on early automobiles with sad bug-eye headlights. The kids have dirty cheeks, wear tattered clothing, and are rail thin. Heading west for a better future, they probably didn't find it, or their car broke down before they got there.

I connect to their story of westward migration not because of dire economics, but because the meaning of living and working in New York had dried up for me. My hometown with infinite possibilities didn't feel possible anymore. My career was at a dead end and my event programming experience was useless in a software programming world. So I am making a modern flight to greener pastures on similarly antiquated equipment. I feel fortunate for today's technology like GPS and credit cards, and I'm grateful for roadside snacks like frosted root beer and pulled pork sandwiches.

By 1938 the route was fully paved, allowing cars to go faster. With speed came deadly accidents. Highway patrols formed to impose order. Engineering professors at Oklahoma State University developed the parking meter to force turnover in towns flooded with parked cars.

After WWII, railroads couldn't keep up with the demand for interstate commerce. Truck traffic used Route 66 to reach consumers more efficiently. Attractions sprung up next to gas stations, motels, and restaurants. The good times were rolling, but not fast enough.

A speedier network was needed and with fewer access points. The Eisenhower administration developed an interstate system without stop signs or small towns in the way. It would also speed evacuations in case of a military attack on

America. Route 66 went from a model highway to an outdated alleyway. In 1984, the interstate bypassed the final Route 66 town of Williams, Arizona. The Mother Road was stripped of signage and decertified, and her pavement has been cracking ever since.

Few Americans still take Route 66 road trips, but foreign fascination is for real. There are Route 66 driving clubs and festivals overseas. Europeans, Asians, and Australians visit the dying towns of McLean, Texas, and Ash Fork, Arizona, where I would never stop had I an engine. A store clerk in Seligman tells me that thirty international tour buses a day stop en route to the Grand Canyon.

Maybe it's more fun by car or motorcycle. Route 66 taps into a driving dream that combines freedom and exploration with the ease of stepping on a gas pedal. I have two pedals but no gas. Riding the Mother Road on a bicycle will be a bitch, but at least she captures the spirit of small town America that gave ordinary people a chance to own a business doing what they loved. Figuring out what that business is for me and where I can start it makes traveling this road worth the rough conditions.

Route 66 is known for quirky roadside attractions. One of these is a concrete sperm whale that looks like a mini golf obstacle on steroids. The Blue Whale's mouth hangs open and you can walk on the tongue into its belly. Water slides poke out of the cheeks into a pond where swimming is prohibited. It's not much to look at, but in the age of Instagram, it draws people from all over.

My host in Tulsa warns that biking on 66 into the city is dangerous, and she offers to pick me up at the whale. After riding twelve consecutive days across Missouri and into Kansas and northeast Oklahoma, I have no shame accepting a ride. Then I'll see how Route 66 was meant to be experienced—in a car.

I have only a dozen miles until the Blue Whale. For once, I'm ahead of schedule and take a break on the grass outside a gas station called QuikTrip. Pleased with my progress, I lie down and look at the sky. Before I move on, I squirt more sunscreen and rub it in. Then, out of habit, I squeeze each tire. The front is firm and the back collapses in my fingers. The tire feels flat. The tire looks flat. But the tire cannot be flat. I've done the tire squeeze countless times. Multiple times per day. Just to make sure.

"Nope, no problems whatsoever!" I'd say when people asked me how the bike was holding up. That answer got more impressive at 200 miles...500 miles...in Pittsburgh...after one month... Cincinnati...1,000 miles...Louisville...St. Louis...two months... the Katy Trail...1,500 miles! But here on Route 66, where some got their kicks, I get my first flat at mile 1,760 in Claremore, Oklahoma.

I spin around in circles and fall down on the grass. I left New York without any tools or know-how. The gas station has an air compressor, which I'm not sure how to use because I'm not good at mechanical stuff. But Haskell knows. He saw me walking this strange bike and comes over to help. He's twenty-four and has a trim goatee and sparkling blue eyes. The tire won't hold air. I can't make it to the whale thing, so Haskell invites me for a "healthy shake" at a nutrition club while I wait for my Tulsa host.

"Hope to see you there!" he says with a smile, handing me a business card. This is the Oklahoma hospitality I will come to know and love.

I ride the flat to a nearby shopping center and find 6:19 Nutrition, which must relate to some Bible verse. I can't peer inside because one-way mirror film is on the window. I slowly open the door, bracing for the unknown. Guys are jumping on couches and shooting mini basketballs into a hoop on a door frame. Others gather around a bar drinking shakes. Containers for Herbalife24 are stacked in pyramids on the wall.

"Jeffrrrrreeeeey!" calls Haskell from behind the bar. Others echo my name and cheer my arrival.

I don't know what I've walked into, but the positive vibes make my heart beat faster. Haskell silences the room and introduces me as the guy who's biking from New York, which is probably obvious because I brought the bike with its license plate inside. I get my choice of unsweetened tea—peach, melon, or Skittles, the bestseller. I meet the owner, Alex, a Tulsa firefighter who quit to open this franchise. Business is great. His customers love the product and he loves them. Haskell shows me side-by-side pics and the difference is clear. Husky Haskell at 220 pounds is drunk, fat, and wearing a Happy New Year's hat. Happy Haskell has slimmed to 180 and looks sober and healthy.

"Jeffrey, Herbalife can truly change your life if you will just let it," he whispers, giving me a large container with his favorite flavor inside.

An attractive young woman tells me she gained six pounds of muscle. Another guy says he lost forty pounds. Have I walked into an infomercial? I guess I believe them. They're not paid actors. They're standing right in front of me, nice people trying to improve through better choices. I didn't think people in Middle America cared about what they ate, which seems to be a conveyor line of energy drinks, soda, fried food, and unholy amounts of beef. But here in a random Oklahoma shopping center, I find an oasis of wellness.

As I wait for my Tulsa host, Haskell takes out a measuring tape and wraps it around my waist, chest, bicep, and thigh. Then comes the weigh-in on a smart scale. I step on and he starts scribbling.

"How'd I do, boss?"

"Your numbers are really good! Nine percent body fat is great and your metabolic age is twelve...that's my age too!" he chimes, although in fact he's twelve calendar years younger.

I'm not buying it. "Even after all that fried catfish, one-pound cheeseburgers, and onion rings?"

"The numbers don't lie," Haskell smiles.

The only troubling stat is 2.5 percent visceral fat coating my organs. I blame the chocolate shakes, but refuse to reform. Winter is coming and I'll need the insulation.

CHAPTER 18

WHERE EAST, WEST, AND SOUTH MEET

Oklahoma. It's not the Midwest like neighboring Missouri. It's not the South or Southwest like next door Arkansas and New Mexico. It's not the High Plains like Kansas or Nebraska. And certainly don't call it Texas. Oklahoma is right in the middle of American geography, yet not part of anything. Old maps label part of the state No Man's Land. To those not familiar with Oklahoma, this still sounds perfectly correct.

I have no idea what to expect from Tulsa. I can't picture the city or who would live there. Oil barons, cowboys, Indians, rednecks, hipsters, frackers, tumbleweeds? With no professional sports teams or famous landmarks, Tulsa is a beige canvas in my mind. I paint a black oil derrick in the middle and wait to see what comes next.

The first thing I notice is the skyline. There are skyscrapers. A few look historic. As a New Yorker, I assume that's where the action is and roll downtown on my newly fixed tire. Lines on the road are so faded that I can't tell the direction of one-way streets. Some intersections don't even have painted crosswalks.

This is downtown? I ride in the middle of the road because there are no moving cars. Sure, it's Saturday and the office workers are home, but where are the millennial urban revivalists? The ones I met in Pittsburgh, Cincinnati, and St. Louis. Darkened storefronts advertise Coney dogs, baked potatoes, cabbage rolls, and Frito pies. Is this what Tulsans eat for lunch? What decade did I fall into?

Once the Oil Capital of the World, Tulsa has been left in the dust. It's not even the capital of Oklahoma. Even during boom times, Tulsa was not a petroleum paradise for everyone. In 1921, the worst racial violence in US history destroyed a thriving African American neighborhood called Greenwood, home to Black Wall Street. About 70 percent of homes and 100 percent of businesses were looted and burned during the Tulsa Race Massacre. The exact death toll is unknown, but up to 300 people, mostly Black men, were murdered by a white mob and dumped into the river and unmarked graves. I didn't learn about this in AP US History. Neither did students in Tulsa public schools, according to my host, Cathy Essley, who picked me up at the nutrition cafe.

"I grew up going to TPS and have taught in public schools for twelve years," she tells me. "It was never taught, but I heard about it from my grandfather who lived through it." T.J. Essley was a first sergeant with the Oklahoma National Guard who happened to be at the armory when violence first broke out. He fended off a mob of white townsmen from seizing guns and ammo to use against the Blacks in Greenwood, and then he helped move a passenger train to safety that was caught in the crossfire.

Downtown Tulsa today is much calmer. Empty parking lots are everywhere. A Katy Trail supporter gave me a button that said, "Asphalt is the last crop." Nothing grows in parking lots. I feel like I'm in a nuclear exclusion zone. Cathy said the police didn't use to patrol here on weekends because there was nobody to protect. Now in 2015, the downtown core has rebounded to almost 4,000 residents. That's smaller than most towns I've biked through, yet the city's overall population is similar to Minneapolis and Cleveland.

Countri Bike is locked outside a coffee and cocktail bar called Hodges Bend. I'm across the street on the patio of East Village Bohemian Pizza keeping an eye on it. An orphaned crust is all that's left of my Mount Vesuvius made with spicy *soppressata*, roasted jalapenos, and buffalo mozzarella. A guy my age exits the bar. He sees the bike, looks around, sees me, and jogs over.

"Hey! Is that your bike?"

I smile and nod as the waitress drops the check on the table. He scoops it up.

"I'm going to pay for his meal," he announces, whipping out a credit card. I trade stunned looks with the server.

Clutching a copy of Mary Shelley's *Frankenstein*, Mark Perkins is "dorking out" by underlining timeless passages. It's Monday and he's playing hooky from lawyering. I tell Mark how I'm biking west to find a new home and he explains why he, a native Okie, likes it here.

"It's exciting to be in a city that's in the building phase rather than already built out. To be part of that building is really energizing." He then says something that I will repeat to others down the road, "Tulsa is like the younger brother of Austin that no one knows about."

Cool people are treated like overstock in Austin, Brooklyn, Portland, and San Francisco. But Tulsa? The vacancy light is glowing. Stuff hasn't been done here. The city is thirsty for ideas, and business opportunities are everywhere.

My next Tulsa host is a petite yoga instructor with a sweet, light laugh. Margot and I stay up late chatting at her kitchen table that is papered with floor plans and spreadsheets for a yoga studio in a historic building with rooftop space.

"I'm twenty-five and have no idea what I'm doing," she laughs while twirling a pencil. I can't help her crunch the numbers (math!), but I tell her that she's going to succeed. She's following her talent and passion. I'm following my talent (bike commuting?) and passion (traveling) and doing well on the road. Just one flat so far.

Margot says two friends, also in their twenties, just opened a bakery. It's a huge storefront in the Arts District with sea salt and chocolate chip cookies that are love at first bite. Tables overlook Main Street's low brick buildings. If they can dream it and do it, why can't Margot? And why can't I? I want a chance to create a place that has permanence. Not the events I planned for months only to disappear after an evening. That job gave me an income, but it never gave me a purpose.

What if I could create a home on the road for travelers to eat, drink, chat, and meet locals? I have little business experience and even less in savings. It's a bold thought, but I've already proven my determination by riding a Citi Bike to Oklahoma.

People move to New York or LA to follow their dreams. I'm already from NYC. It didn't work out for me. People there trample over one another chasing too few pathways to success. At networking events I was sized up based on where I lived and worked. What could I do for them, they wondered. In Tulsa, people ask what they can do for me.

Four days here and I leave with more contacts than I have active in NYC. These aren't just names on my phone. They're Tulsans with a genuine interest in me as a person. Yes, it's Oklahoma—no man's land—but something special is happening here and the chemistry is hard to ignore.

That first morning, fresh off the ferry to New Jersey, I stared at the Atlantic Ocean. I couldn't project my dreams onto the blank horizon. Now I'm looking at a canvas called Tulsa and a faint sketch is taking shape.

I bike over the Arkansas River, which looks more like a muddy puddle. I don't realize it then, but I've just entered the West for real this time. The Gateway Arch in St. Louis is symbolic and so was the Wheeling Suspension Bridge 600 miles before it, but for me, the dividing line between East and West runs through Tulsa. Leaving here, the dirt gets redder. Men wear cowboy hats and boots. Pickup trucks go from heavy duty to super duty. And the wind blows harder. Today it's driving against me, but I don't mind. I've got new clothes.

Last night I ended up at a bicycle dive bar called Soundpony. Stools were made out of bike chains and handlebars. Dusty racing jerseys hung from the ceiling. Dried out hot dogs spun in a warmer behind the bar. I loved everything about this place, especially the people.

The owner goes by Woz. He's forty-something with silver-streaked hair, a lanky frame, and oversized glasses. Woz and Bikey, a burly guy with a shaved head and white goatee, welcome me like family. They give me Soundpony socks and a racing jersey with neon stripes that make me look like a European ambulance. I also get stickers for my bike and an iron-on patch of the Soundpony, a winged horse with a squeeze horn for a nose. I'm happier than a ten-year-old birthday boy.

The party gets bigger when four cross-country bikers walk in. People like me and going my way! People who know what I'm going through day after day. Three of them could be boy band brothers with their young looks and electric blond hair. (Coincidentally, Hanson is from Tulsa. Their recording studio is down the block.) Friends from school, they just picked up a fourth an hour ago outside of Walmart. I imagine this pudgy black-haired biker is their drummer. These guys are full of carefree energy and eat peanut butter nonstop. They bike fast, far, and at night. They plan to bike thirty more miles tonight, but things are getting rather festive. Bikey is buying us shots with cheap beer chasers and telling stories from when he was on the road back in the day. The boys and I are drinking it up in our matching bike jerseys like it's an initiation into Soundpony fraternity. Other Sunday night regulars ply us with more drinks and well wishes. Biking across America has felt like being a lone wolf, but at Soundpony, I've found temporary protection with this bicycle-friendly pack.

Leaving Tulsa I'm back to wolf status, but at least I have new cycling clothes. I got plenty of advice on the best way out of town, but forgot it all in the happy fog of last night. Google Maps routes me onto an old alignment of Route 66. I cross a small rusting bridge with a brick deck. Markings on the road have worn away. There's no traffic, so I slalom to avoid big cracks in the pavement. The area is wooded and trailer homes are set back from the road. I have no idea where I am except that I'm not far enough. Headwinds have slowed me to six miles per hour. It's one o'clock and I'm worried I won't reach Stroud, the halfway stop to Oklahoma City, before nightfall.

I stop to stretch and check Instagram. There's no shoulder, so I park the bike on the edge of the pavement and walk around the grass, which is covered with autumn leaves. A dark battered pickup truck pulls up. A white man in a tank top is behind the wheel. The passenger window is down. I look at him, ready to answer common questions. Nope, the bike isn't electric. Yup, I really rode it from New York. Nah, there's not a baby in the back.

I don't hear any words, just his boiling voice. His blue eyes are like ice cubes of frozen anger. Tattoos run up and down both arms. I don't notice the teardrops inked on his cheek.

"I'm sorry, sir. I just stopped on the side of this road. I'm not trying to be in the way," I say one octave higher than normal. My soft apology enrages him. He spews curses at me for being on a bicycle and then smokes the tires and screeches off.

I'm in shock. I don't believe what just happened, but a tire trail tattoos the road and burnt rubber lingers in the air. I pace around the bike to walk off the shakes. I'm alone and unarmed, except for that baby Louisville Slugger buried in the trailer.

My ears perk up. A vehicle ahead comes tearing around the bend. It's the same truck. I'm on the grass behind the bike, watching it come closer. It's gunning right for me. My feet won't move.

Squealing brakes snap me back into my body. The driver's door is just feet away.

"I told you get the FUCK off the road!" the man screams with popping neck veins. "You're in the same DAMN spot! I told you fucker to get outta here, you fuckin' idiot!"

I don't remember if I say anything. I don't remember what else he says. The sound is off and life is in slow motion. I watch the door open as his thin but muscular frame emerges. He reaches for me with arms that pop out like a jack-in-the-box. One hand grabs my Soundpony bike jersey. The other clenches into a fist. I know what's coming but I can't stop it. Knuckles smash into my mouth. I stumble back, waiting for the pain. I watch him go after the bike, screaming as he kicks it over. He then gets back in the truck and takes off.

I touch my lip to feel for missing teeth and pull my hand away. It's covered in blood.

Two sheriff's deputies from Creek County walk in with tight brown pants and pressed shirts. One has darker skin and jet black hair, maybe a citizen of the Creek Nation. The other is white with buzzed blond hair. I'm in the emergency room in a town I've never heard of and can't pronounce.

"Sap-uh-loop-ah?" I ask.

"Sapulpa," says the white officer. "Welcome to Oklahoma." They both laugh.

As my attacker fled, a couple in a mini pickup stopped. The wife handed me napkins to mop up the streaming blood while her husband called 911. I declined an ambulance and took their offer to drive me to the emergency room. My bike and trailer went in the back and we sat three across in the front. To see the damage for myself, I took a selfie and, after some hesitation, posted it to Instagram.

The deputies ask questions and I give answers, the best I can with an icepack on my mouth. They especially want to know about the truck, but all I know is that it was old and blue, maybe some wood planks hanging out the back.

"Sounds like every other truck in Oklahoma," one officer says as they share another laugh.

Make or model I have no clue. People in NYC don't drive pickups. It would be like a tourist saying the cabbie who hit her drove a yellow car. And in the heat of the moment you can't pause reality to zoom in and copy down a plate number.

The officers leave and a doctor comes in. He introduces himself as Dr. No. I hope I'm hearing this wrong. He says that I need stitches. I hope I'm hearing that wrong too. Dr. No turns away and I hear the scratch of medical instruments on the metal tray.

I squirm in the gurney. Should I tell No "no!" and go back to Tulsa for treatment? Or ask for another doctor not named after a James Bond villain? Dr. Noh is Vietnamese. After the fall of Saigon, thousands of South Vietnamese refugees fled to America and some were resettled in Oklahoma. I take another picture of my face to see what I look like. Dried blood stains my chin. The gash is a jagged red line that cuts across the width of my lip and into the stubble above it. Dr. Noh sews four stitches to close the wound.

My new friend Jason is here. With kind blue eyes and a shaved head, his presence reassures me. Jason, a forty-four-year-old law partner, was my third and final host in Tulsa. "If you need anything, just text," he said this morning as I pedaled away from his red brick home near Utica Square. Jason left work early to get me, taking his partner's company van so that it could fit the bike.

On our way back to Tulsa, I have to make a phone call. To my parents. I'm dreading this conversation, which is why I've saved it for last. My mom answers the landline and, in a familiar routine, hollers for my dad to pick up. I circle around the news, saying how you have good days and bad days. My mom knows something is off and pounces for details. I recount the highlights as calmly as possible.

"Did you see a plastic surgeon?" she implores, hours too late.

Actually, I didn't think of that. Dr. Noh said that when it comes to stitches, the sooner the better. I'd have to wait at a medical center in Tulsa and incur more fees. I've already paid $200 for something I didn't want.

"Jeffrey, oh my God, it's your FACE!" she shrieks. "I think you need to come home now. You need to stop biking around Kansas or wherever and just stop this."

"Mom, I'm in Tulsa and I like it here. The people are nice. They're gonna take care of me."

By now the selfie has made the rounds on social media. Tulsans rally to my side. I get offers from free beer to an escorted ride out of town. Along with the swelling on my face, my Instagram following gets a bump. Woz from Soundpony texts asking if he can share my number with a reporter who contacted him.

A TV reporter and her cameraman meet me at Guthrie Green across from News On 6 studios. Meagan Farley is about my age and has no ring on her finger either. She's animated and talks fast. I'm sensing an East Coast vibe. Turns out Meagan is from New Jersey. She spent a year at ABC in Manhattan and then at stations in Topeka, Roanoke, and Albany. She then jumped to Tulsa, which she loves and wants to make her forever home. After the interview, she invites me to lunch at Chimera coffee shop the next day.

Jason drives me to his home so I can rest. His partner brings back Lebanese takeout for dinner. We eat while watching play-off baseball that leads into the local news. The saying is true: if it bleeds, it leads. My bloody selfie is the backdrop to the top story.

I welcome the coverage in Tulsa but don't appreciate it elsewhere. The attack drowns out the narrative of why I'm doing this. It's also bad press for Oklahoma, which already has a poor reputation. Both NYC tabloids print a blurb. The story spreads on Reddit and cycling forums. It's trending on Gothamist, which links to my blog. Internet trolls devour the article and have a field day in the comments.

"I bet the driver passed to [sic] close to douche-canoe. Douche-canoe gave the hillbilly the finger or something and thus we end up with a bleeding douche-canoe."

"Looks like a really bad cold sore to me. I think he faked this assault to explain why he got injury [sic] on his upper lip."

"Holy shit, dude's writing is insufferably self-indulgent. Between that and an attention seeking, pointless trek across the country with a Citibike, I think the attacker should get a mulligan for the punch."

"The pickup truck guy had probably been following him on Instagram and had finally had enough."

"Yeah seriously. And his self aggrandizing Instagram posts. Gross. He does sound super punchable."

"So he stole the bike and took it cross-country just because? Fuck this guy, glad he got clocked in the face."

"Seething redneck on meth meets NYC douchenozzle. A tornado showing up right as they met would have been the perfect ending."

"Another self-entitled, hipster idiot makes the news again. First he steals a Citi Bike, then he creates, then attempts to "diffuse" a situation by behaving condescendingly toward what sounds like a real working man, while thinking his self-important, pseudo-superior social status will save him; it's only surprising he wasn't punched out sooner."

The "real working man," it turns out, is a career criminal. His rap sheet has assault and battery with a dangerous weapon, assault and battery of a police officer (twice), kidnapping, and first-degree burglary.

The next day, my phone rings with a blocked number from Sapulpa. A detective is on the line. He wants to meet in an hour to show me a lineup. I'm walking the bike through Brookside where skinny moms in Lululemon have brunch and shop at stores like Lululemon. A lady apologizes to me through the open window of her luxury SUV. Two shopkeepers come outside to wish me well. I'm heading to R Bar to meet a new friend. He made a humble request on Instagram that I couldn't refuse: to shake my hand.

Samuel is a twenty-one-year-old barista, soft-spoken and caring. We're having a free beer on the patio courtesy of someone else who recognized me. Everybody in Tulsa is talking about this story. A portly detective arrives in a pink polo, shattering my stereotype of law enforcement, even if a gun is holstered to his hip.

He hands me a printout with the mugshots of eight white men. My heart is pounding. I want justice. I want to find the guy who hurt me for no reason. I quickly scan the photos, hoping one will jump out.

"No, none of them," I say after looking at each face more closely.

"OK, what about these?" he says, putting another paper on the table. More choices! My heart races as I hold my breath.

"THIS ONE!" I cry, slamming my finger onto a face that is hauntingly familiar.

"What about that one makes you think it's him?"

"Uhh...the hairline, the nose, the eyes. Definitely those eyes. I've seen them before."

"Well, you're right," he says.

"Wait. What? What do you mean I'm right?"

The guy I pointed to is in jail. His name is Franklin, alias Frankenstein. He's thirty-seven. Police nabbed him last night after he tried to murder a couple he was living with near where I was attacked. He took a baseball bat to smack the woman in the face. She ran bleeding to a neighbor's house for help. Frankenstein then bashed her boyfriend so hard that the bat broke into three pieces. Then he got a double-sided axe and kept swinging. When the girlfriend came back with her neighbor, Franklin pushed a gun into the neighbor's face and broke his glasses before getting away in a dark blue truck. When the police caught him, he confessed to everything. His only remorse was for not killing his friends, who remain in critical condition.

Samuel and I trade stunned looks. I was attacked by a real-life axe murderer. I bike back to Jason's house. His law firm has an extra ticket for corporate night at Oktoberfest. Under white tents, people roam around drinking liters of beer from plastic steins. They do the Chicken Dance, stomping on picnic tables to the beat of a German polka.

I wash down antibiotics with a Marshall's dunkel lager. Channel 2 calls and wants my reaction to the arrest. They dispatch a reporter and cameraman to interview me. The gory details make me the top story for the second night in a row. I'm officially Tulsa famous.

Jason says he's driving to Oklahoma City the day after tomorrow and asks if I want a lift. I sure do. Even with that psychopath in jail, I don't want to go back through the scene of the crime, and it's supposed to rain for the next two days anyway.

OKC is far more developed than Tulsa, but something feels off. Tulsa was built with purpose while OKC is spread out and disconnected. I visit the memorial to the 1995 Oklahoma City bombing, where in black sweatpants and light blue zip-up I'm mistaken for an OKC Thunder recruit. I'm correctly identified by cyclists at Elemental Coffee where a TV reporter happens to be on a break. I make the local news again.

Leaving my Oklahoma network behind, I carry Sooner State scars into Texas.

CHAPTER 19

CROSSING THE TEXAS PANHANDLE

Are There Ghosts in Groom?

It's Halloween and I'm about to do something scary—bike fifty-nine miles on a Citi Bike from Elk City, Oklahoma, to Shamrock, Texas. I'll need the luck of the Irish to make it by nightfall.

The day begins in a motel lobby pulling the rain cover over the bike trailer when Shane, a native Okie, walks in. He sees my bike and introduces himself as doing something in the oil industry. Typical Oklahoman—works in energy and kindly energetic.

Shane is a triathlete. He invites me outside to see his bike on the back of a Chevy Suburban. Not all bikes are created equal. Triathlete bikes are light, aerodynamic, and expensive. Shane's streamlined bike is a delicate appendage on a bloated SUV. I imagine the pleasure of floating on a bike thirty pounds lighter than my anvil on wheels. I'd get to California tomorrow.

"I gotta admit, your rig is pretty sweet," I say. "Must ride like a magic carpet."

"Even better," he says.

Shane starts talking about blended forks and brakes. Shimano shifters. Aero positions. Crankset something. I nod and drop "nice" or "cool" every so often, but have no idea what he's talking about. It's like when someone asks if you've seen a certain movie when such and such happens and you lie just to keep the conversation going. Shane continues to speak in bike parts as I steer us inside so I can settle the bill.

"Your bike looks more expensive than the truck," I joke.

"Just about $10,000," Shane says with a grin.

The sleepy desk clerk comes to life. "Ten *thousand* dollars for a *bi*-cycle," she gasps. "Well, I'll be!"

With that kind of money maybe she'd pursue her own passion rather than watch strangers come and go while the hands of time tick around in circles. Spending a fortune on something she hasn't tried since childhood prompts her to ask questions about our bikes.

When traveling alone, camaraderie can arise anywhere if you're open to it, even a Motel 6 lobby. Shane and I share war stories from the road, specifically Oklahoma roads. I was punched in the face in Sapulpa. Shane was hit on the helmet with a beer bottle in OKC. Clasping her hands, the desk clerk is all ears.

"If you get hit, you gotta hit back. So I maced the hell out of him!" he laughs. "I rode away, not sure if he called the police."

"So, you carry mace when you ride?" I ask.

"I carry mace and pepper mace. One for the dogs who get on my bad side and one for the humans who get on my bad side."

He's also been pelted with golf balls. A passenger in a moving pickup truck once tried to slug his friend with a baseball bat. Thanks to a helmet mirror the cyclist ducked at the right time.

None of this is making me feel better after my recent assault. How will I protect myself next time? The downside to mace is that you can spray yourself in the heat of the moment or the wind can blow against you.

As for dogs in angry pursuit, I still haven't found a solution despite the options. Mace. Rocks. Water guns filled with lemon juice. I hear that air horns work best and don't require bull's-eye aim to hit a moving animal. The shocking noise stops dogs in their tracks.

Sometimes handheld accessories don't fend off danger. They cause it. Earlier in the summer, just south of Elk City, a distracted driver killed a cyclist. Shane brings it up, but I already know the story. It was in the *New York Post* a week before I left. The article grabbed me. Patrick Wanninkhof was working as a teacher in the Bronx and going cross-country as part of a Bike & Build charity ride. He got killed in a state I planned on riding through.

Little did I know then that I would ride so near where Patrick died. Sarah Morris of Cordell, Oklahoma, was looking at her phone and "didn't see" him and a friend resting on the side of the road. That was her explanation for ending a life twenty-five years young. She was charged with first-degree manslaughter, a felony. The other cyclist with Patrick suffered serious injuries.

Back on the road, I'm closing in on the Texas border when my eyes start playing tricks. Something small and black is ahead. I think it's a dog because it's weaving back and forth, but it seems larger than an animal. Maybe a motorcycle, but it's going too slowly. It's getting bigger, which means I'm faster. Someone walking? No, someone riding a bicycle. Someone like me!

An exciting goal is suddenly in reach. I'm determined to catch whoever this is. It's lonely out here and I want a bike buddy. As I get closer I notice something else. Long black hair. It's not a man—it's a woman!

She's weaving side-to-side with fatigue. I surprise her with a thundering hello. She turns with a jolt, but I'm the one who is shocked. She's Asian. Her name is Jane and she's Korean. I've never been to Korea, but I love the food. My friend Miell, a Korean American, does all the ordering. I just sit there eating *ban-chan*, little plates of spicy and pickled side dishes, waiting for the entrees to arrive.

As my closest college friend, Miell and I have been through good and bad times. I held her hand while we walked to the dean's office when she was on the verge of getting expelled for poor grades. The dean told me to wait outside, but Miell wanted me in. She cried on my shoulder when they told her she could stay at Dartmouth.

On that frozen January day in New Hampshire, Miell seemed far from a successful future. Struggling with family issues and on academic probation, she took an extra year to graduate as a brain sciences major. She wanted to go to med school and become a doctor to prove her worth to her traditional Korean parents, but she never got beyond studying for the MCAT.

Fifteen years later, Miell runs her own standardized test tutoring company in Princeton, New Jersey, just beyond the gates of that elite university. She manages about thirty private students a week. She even has a princeton.edu email for running a free college prep course for underrepresented and underserved high schoolers. Failure can sometimes lead to great success.

Miell's hair is long and black like Jane's. I suddenly miss my friends and the beauty of New England—winding roads through green mountains that lead to small towns with white fences and American flags. Flat and dusty Erick, Oklahoma, is not Hanover, New Hampshire. And Jane is not Miell. Jane and I have nothing in common except for being on bicycles, which maybe is a lot in common in rural Oklahoma.

Our bicycles are the only traffic in any direction. Erick is the last chance for food or drinks until dinner in Shamrock. I suggest that we pull over to find lunch. The town cafe is closed as is the Roger Miller Museum about the musician who grew up here. That leaves Puckett's Food Store as the only option.

We lean our bikes on the side of the building and I peel off layers. I'm wrapped in accessories with the American flag to prove my patriotism while hiding my skin from the sun. Jane is in all black, including her headscarf. That's good for urban fashion but bad for road visibility.

We walk into the store. It happens to be Halloween, which hopefully softens the stares. The store is silent except for a price scanner's beep. I get chocolate milk, pepper jack cheese, and pretzels. Jane's having a sports drink that looks like anti-freeze and two junk food all-stars: Oreos and Pringles. As we eat on a bench in the shade, I probe for details about my new traveling partner. Jane is alone, I know. Jane is Korean, I know. Jane lives in Korea? I didn't know that.

"What are you doing in the US?" I ask.

"I'm riding a bike across the states," she says.

"Yes, I can see that," I laugh. "Umm...this is a pretty big country. Why on Earth did you choose it? Korea or Japan would be easier. God knows they have more careful drivers." I remember a video from the 2011 tsunami where Japanese motorists, moments before being swallowed by a wall of water, used turn signals. In America, turn signals are a sign of weakness.

"I wanted a challenge after I finished school. So I wanted to bike across the states," Jane says, explaining how she started in New York and is following Route 66 to LA just like me.

"Your parents must be worried sick," I respond. Mine are and at least I'm white, male, and English is my first language.

She nods silently.

"So, after you finish, you'll go back to Korea and get a job?"

"No. I am going to university."

"No, you just finished school," I say, correcting her.

"I finished high school. Next I go to university."

High school? Oh my gosh, she just finished high school and is biking across America. Alone. A woman. Asian. On the edge of Texas and Oklahoma. I'm on the edge of my seat.

"Are you staying in motels or doing Warm Showers?" I ask.

"Sometimes I stay with host, but I camp outside people's house."

"What people?"

"I knock on the door."

"Whose door? Jane! What the hell are you doing?"

"The nicest door," she says calmly.

I spill chocolate milk on my lap. This young woman knocks on the doors of strangers and camps in their yard. Sometimes she gets invited inside. Jane is far braver than I'll ever be. Yesterday it rained nonstop. I sheltered in place at Motel 6 and visited Elk City's Route 66 Museum. What did Jane do? She rode all day in the fucking rain. I'm worried about the gradual onset of winter. She's gotta make LA before her visa expires. She can't stop, won't stop.

We finish our snacks and saddle up. We're both heading to Shamrock and keep riding together. My heart beats faster. Having a companion quickens the crossing of these empty miles.

The last town in Oklahoma is Texola, which is a lil' bit Texas and a lil' bit...*Olahoma*? Actually, it's a whole lotta nothing. Weeds burst through cracks in the road. Overgrown grass and abandoned houses are right out of a zombie apocalypse film set.

On cue, snarling dogs appear, too many to count while moving. This canine committee isn't out to welcome us.

Jane starts screaming. She's scared of dogs and the ones patrolling Texola are a bloodthirsty subspecies. Curled lips show sharp teeth ready for their first taste of Korean and New Yorker. I'm going full speed ahead trying to outpace them. Jane lags behind, about to be ripped from her ride and eaten alive. Then I realize I missed the turn out of Texola because our avenue of escape looked like a dead end. To go back, we must go through the dogs. I start screaming too.

I don't remember how we did it, but the dogs of Texola never got a lick. Jane is cursing at me in Korean, but then I show her something that brings a smile. It's a Welcome to Texas sign. Like everything else in Texas, the sign is huge. It optimistically asks motorists to "Drive friendly, the Texas way." I hope they drive friendlier than in Oklahoma.

Jane and I enter Texas. Specifically, the Texas Panhandle, an empty box that sits atop the Lone Star State like a cowboy hat. The Panhandle looks small compared to the rest of the state, but don't be fooled. There's a lot of land up here, including a county that's larger than Rhode Island.

We roll into Shamrock along Route 66. Feeling increasingly loyal to the Mother Road, I pick the Route 66 Inn. Out of politeness and sincerity, I offer Jane the extra bed in my room. Out of fear or formality she declines, but promises to text me once she finds the nicest door to knock on.

I'm starving. The motel clerk recommends Big Vern's for dinner. I don't know who Vern is, but a big steak within walking distance sounds perfect for celebrating biking to Texas. A fake covered wagon straddles the pump stand at Big Vern's, an old gas station. Pickup trucks are the vehicle of choice in the parking lot. It looks like the kind of place where they toss you out on your ass if you're not wearing denim and cowboy boots.

In a neon yellow windbreaker and electric blue sneakers, I'm not rockin' the Panhandle look. My stomach tightens walking alone to an open table, but insecurity melts away with the first bite of ribeye so buttery that no sauce is needed. Twelve ounces for twenty-four dollars is affordable and delicious.

Jane found a place to crash and we start texting. Tonight the clocks turn back, robbing us of an hour of daylight. That means we need to leave earlier and ride faster. Tomorrow has one uphill climb and seven miles on the interstate, so I want to get an early start.

Jane agrees until she realizes it's Sunday and church is at nine o'clock. She continues to amaze me, but such a delay is a deal-breaker. Jane bikes more slowly, and leaving after ten, we'll never make it to Groom before dark, no matter how hard she prays.

I head out on my own. Route 66 is an empty frontage road along Interstate 40 where cars and trucks hurtle through the Panhandle. There's nothing of interest on the horizon, but there's plenty of concern right in front of me. Pavement cracks are getting worse and loose puncturevine thorns threaten my tires.

It's a straight shot to McLean, the only hope for hot food till Groom. McLean's Route 66 attraction is the Devil's Rope Museum. I would stop to learn about barbed wire, but it closed for the season yesterday. Today is November 1. Clocks fall back and businesses are going into off-season mode. Winter is moving faster than I am.

I soothe my anxiety with fried pickles and a milkshake at a greasy spoon on Main Street. In walks a couple with a foreign accent. They're from Britain and sit down at the counter one stool away from me. They must be Route 66 heritage travelers. The husband lobs comments at the waitress, hoping one will strike a conversation. She has other things on her plate, so I respond for her in my head. But when he complains about how difficult it is to drive when there's nothing to see, I can't keep quiet.

"Hey bloke, if you think driving is so hard, try the Panhandle on a bicycle," I sneer while chewing on a straw. They don't believe me until I take them outside and show Countri Bike locked to the railing of a vacant storefront. The guy then photographs me like another odd Route 66 roadside attraction.

The next settlement is Alanreed. I stop to look around an abandoned Texaco station. Dust decades thick coats the interior. This place was the real deal, pumping refined Texas tea into 1950s and '60s muscle cars. The one open business welcomes visitors with a sign—Alanreed City Limits: 52 people, 104 dogs, 88 cats, 2 skunks, and a few snakes. The store functions as a gas station, convenience store, gift shop, motel, and post office rolled into one. Less convenient is the fact that Route 66 disappears, leaving me with two terrible options: trespass on a dirt road through Mr. Johnson's Ranch or ride seven miles on the interstate shoulder. The ranch option is tempting, but I know Texans take their property—and their guns—seriously.

The interstate has dangers of its own. All those cars. All those trucks. I've never seen a speed limit of 75 mph or biked on the interstate. Is it even legal? Yes. No federal laws prohibit bicycles from interstate shoulders, although local statutes can forbid it. For example, biking on interstates is allowed in New Mexico, just not around Albuquerque where frequent access ramps make it dangerous and calmer city streets are plentiful.

There is no public road here except I-40, so I begin my merge onto the shoulder. Are cars freaking out to see me? Because I am, seeing them. I feel their whoosh, which hits my face and rings in my ears. Gone is the safety of the cracked but quiet frontage road. Now I'm on the interstate. Texas is terrifying without Jane's company.

Up ahead, a lifesaver. I pedal into the Gray County Safety Rest Area, which welcomes me with the sign Watch Out For Snakes. Jesus, I can't even let my guard down at a rest stop. Mini grills in the shape of Texas make me wish I had beef and charcoal, but I settle for a pack of Skittles from the vending machine before moving on.

A wide ramp feeds me onto I-40. I'm on the shoulder six feet from semis so large they block out the sun. Biking on the interstate is like jumping into a pool of cold water. You know it's going to suck, but once you're in for a few minutes, it feels fine.

I reach Groom at the magical hour when the sun and sky team up for a vibrant color show. This town's claim to fame is a nineteen-story white cross that soars into cerulean skies. More than a religious symbol, the cross also marks 2,000 miles biked from Manhattan.

Groom has a surprising number of tidy houses. I pass a corner lot where a husband and wife are outside. The garage is open, showing off an organized workbench and American flag on the wall. A golden retriever sits on the lawn. Flames dance around a fire pit. Could this be the quintessential American home?

I slow down to enjoy the beauty of this scene, hoping a cosmic force intervenes so the husband will ask me, "Hey biker guy, wanna stop for a burger? I'm grilling up a storm and my lovely wife made her cinnamon-dusted apple pie—best in the West! Say, friend, you look tired. Why don't ya stay the night on our couch?"

They look at me but don't say anything. I really want apple pie and a couch to crash on. I try to summon Jane's courage to break the ice, but my mouth won't open. I roll away wondering what might have been.

Google reviews for the only motel in town don't live up to the Chalet Inn's fancy name, but I have no choice. Heading toward it, I'm stopped by an oncoming red pickup. Carla asks me if everything is OK. She runs a place over on West First and Choctaw as a boarding house for truckers. She says it's ten dollars for a room. I pedal faster than in Texola just to keep her taillights in sight as dogs bark from every house along the way.

The brick building was once the town's medical clinic, which makes me uneasy. Growing up, I watched too many episodes of *Unsolved Mysteries* hosted by Robert Stack, and this setting surely has a bloody past. Carla remembers getting checkups and vaccines where the kitchen is now. The bathroom was a surgical center with the same drain in the floor. My goosebumps are not going away.

Carla leaves and I'll never see her again. Jane only made it to the rest area and is camping with snakes. I'll never see her again either.

It's deathly quiet. Room doors in the hallway are at disorienting angles like a house of mirrors. Is anyone home? I'm scared either way. In my room, a naked bulb hangs above a bare mattress. The window is boarded up, but the TV gets a few channels. It's one of those giant boxes from the late '90s. I turn it on low just for company. The picture is snowy, but I'm not interested in Sunday night football. Not knowing who last slept here, I spread a clear painter's tarp over the mattress and build a temporary nest with my foam pad and sleeping bag. I'm basically camping indoors.

The shared bathroom sink has simple toiletries belonging to truckers en route to destinations unknown, maybe here. The ghosts of patients past—that I fear will stab me in the shower with a syringe—never materialize.

Groom may be known for a giant cross, but I'll remember the spooky boarding house with free laundry. When you've been wearing the same clothes for this long, a new model washing machine can make your night. Bonus: there's a dryer too. I hope the scent of clean clothing wards off any supernatural predators. I drift into an uneasy sleep with the TV on and the Cowboys trailing the Seahawks late in the fourth quarter.

CHAPTER 20

LAND OF ENTRAPMENT
The Wows and Woes of New Mexico

My back cracks as I wake up on the laundry room floor. It's not a plot twist in a crime novel. It's my reality in Adrian, a no-stoplight town halfway between Chicago and Los Angeles. A sign for Route 66's midpoint does the math for me: 1,139 more miles to go.

Just two dozen miles are left in Texas. I can't wait for a new state. The Panhandle's unforgiving bluster has been brutal on a bicycle. Stop signs were spinning in the wind leaving Amarillo. I took a break at Cadillac Ranch where old cars are planted nose down in a dirt field. The art installation is said to be the hood ornament of Route 66 and its biggest photo op. Tail fins of ten Cadillacs from 1949 to 1963 tilt skyward, now covered in decades worth of spray paint. I had to gently drop the bike over a barbed-wire fence to get it inside. (Anything for Instagram.) Moving on against the headwinds, every revolution required the effort of three. I could walk faster and began pushing the bike, wishing I had buried it at Cadillac Ranch.

I shake off those memories. Today is special. It's my three-month anniversary on the road, and I'm biking sixty-four miles across state lines and time zones. Max and Tyler rustle in their sleeping bags. I'm not alone. I met these cyclists in Oklahoma City. Max and Tyler went to high school together in NYC and graduated from colleges upstate a few months ago. Max, out of SUNY New Paltz, has a fireball of red hair that drops down into a full beard. Tyler, with a degree in geography from Syracuse, is taller with tossed brown hair. Two youngsters delaying entry into the working world for a few months, on a journey into adulthood together.

Our paths overlapped again as last night's temperatures flirted with freezing. There was nowhere to stay, so the owner of the RV park let us sleep inside the laundry room for ten dollars each. We blasted the propane heater overnight, and it's so nice and toasty that I fear we might have overslept. I crack open the door and winter air slaps me awake. A layer of thick clouds hides the typical Texas blue sky.

I tap my phone. Nine seventeen. Shit, we did oversleep. I throw my stuff into the trailer, but they have to pack their panniers more carefully. I wanna get an early start this Sunday while the wind is still sleeping, but the boys *patshke*. This Yiddish word—to mess around—was my dad's favorite expression of frustration on family trips. Now I'm saying it as the de facto dad of our cycling family.

At ten thirty we finally roll away. The only place open is a gas station mart on the western edge of town. The boys want to stop. They need coffee. I don't drink coffee. They need snacks. I already have snacks.

A few miles later, Route 66 vanishes. The interstate is the only option, but I don't know what's ahead—uphill or downhill. Google Maps doesn't show elevation for driving directions and won't route bikes onto the interstate, even though it's legal to be on the shoulder unless otherwise posted. My stomach tightens as we merge onto the shoulder. Tyler leads, Max is in the middle, and I'm the caboose. My new family on wheels gives me more confidence than doing this alone.

For once, the topography tilts in my favor. Max and Tyler turn into black dots. I'm going as fast as I can, but can't catch up. Road construction closes the left lane, forcing vehicles into the right lane next to me on the shoulder. Flatbed trucks with flapping yellow "oversized load" banners carry wind turbine parts. A single blade looks Earth-piercing enormous. I feel as insignificant as an ant, but try to be visible in a reflective neon vest over a neon wind jacket that is trapping moisture. I'm cool on the outside but wet on the inside. My shirt is soggy. My pants are slippery. My feet are cold. I still have a ways to go, but anticipation is building.

Grassy plains give way to shrubby trees and exposed rocks. The Texas Panhandle is losing its grip. Eroded plateaus rise in the distance. A new world lies ahead. For an hour I scan the horizon for the official sign that I've made it to the great American Southwest. Not only is New Mexico a new state, my sixteenth, but also Route 66 reemerges right after the state line. Interstate anxiety is almost over.

A yellow sign straddles the highway like a finish line banner at a marathon. Entering New Mexico and mountain time is my most significant border crossing yet. New Mexico, with Georgia O'Keeffe dreamscapes, spicy food, and native culture is more exotic than Texas, Ohio, New Jersey, or any other state I've passed through.

As a welcome bonus we gain an hour of ride time, although now the sun sets an hour earlier at 5:00 p.m. Max, Tyler, and I regroup at the visitor center. The only food here is vending machine cuisine, so I snack on a red apple and peanut butter, which I also had for dinner last night because there was no food service in Adrian.

Route 66 will take us to Tucumcari, which is still another forty miles away. That's an entire day for me right there. It's time to get going. Once again, the boys jump ahead. I happen upon them seventeen miles later in San Jon. They've just eaten at Taste of India buffet inside a truck stop. Not only are the motel owners out here Indian, but so are the truckers.

San Jon was once a ranching community. Cattle days are over and Route 66 traffic dried up too. A water tower stands over squat homes and three gas stations, one of which is boarded up. We ride out of San Jon together, but I can't keep pace. The boys get smaller and smaller and vanish out of sight. The sky is turning pastel colors. The darkest shade is fast approaching and my energy is low. I stop and stuff two handfuls of M&M's into my mouth, but the boost doesn't last long.

Darkness overtakes me two miles short of Tucumcari. I'm running on fumes. My legs are about to fall off. I'm frequently stopping to rest even though I'm so close. Not even my cheery fight song (*Fight Song* by Rachel Platten) is working.

A rainbow of neon tubes glows ahead. Motel signs were designed to lure weary motorists, and Tucumcari has one of the best-preserved stretches of Route 66. A jumble of flashing colors and shapes calls out comfort.

I've gone almost sixty-five miles, the most on this trip. I think about the distance today and the distance I've gone in three months. Three months exactly today. New York to New Mexico. On a bike—a Citi Bike! Sometimes on the interstate. Mostly alone. And now in the dark. Emotion overtakes exhaustion. I start crying without tears; I'm out of moisture.

The neon sign for the Blue Swallow Motel is a beautiful sight for sore legs. The swallow itself is symbolic. For sailors, this winged blessing is the first sign that land is near. Now I understand how wave-worn seamen felt when spotting a bird. Land ho and home cooking were within reach. I'm in the same boat, except that I'm on a bike and taking myself out for fajitas and margaritas after a long steamy shower. I haven't tasted hot food in thirty hours.

The Blue Swallow is considered the crown jewel of motels along this legendary road. It's also ranked on Tripadvisor's top bargain hotels in America. Me being me, I can't pass up a good deal. Back in San Jon, I called to get a same-day discount. After sleeping on a laundry room floor last night, I'm not camping on cold soil with fresh graduates Max and Tyler. I've done real time in the real world—that's why this whole journey started. Savings are made to spend on moments like these.

I step off the bike and stare at the glowing neon bird. Nancy Mueller opens the door and welcomes me inside with hot tea. She and her husband Kevin bought the motel in 2011. They had been living in Michigan and both lost their jobs in the recession. Unemployment led to soul-searching. Kevin wanted to make a living doing something he enjoyed, and he thought about owning a business. The motel's twelve rooms have been restored to their pastel-era charm. Each comes with an attached private garage. A tight squeeze for a modern car, the garage is a palace for Countri Bike.

Three years after taking over the motel, their two adult children quit their jobs and relocated to help out. I can't imagine moving my family to a town with only 5,000 people. There seems to be more motel rooms than residents. Do people really stop to sleep in Tucumcari?

I got lucky, says Kevin. They're booked solid March to October, turning away as many as a dozen roadies a night. November is slower, and since no one booked the only suite, it's mine for the same price as a regular room.

The Redman Suite is delightful. It's named after Lillian Redman who owned the Blue Swallow with her husband for almost four decades. A sitting room has a couch and fake fireplace that turns out real heat. The bedroom has a tiled alcove with a clawfoot tub stocked with bath salts, a rubber ducky, and a privacy screen. A hot soak is tempting, but impatience moves me to the shower for instant gratification, along with another handful of M&M's.

Morning brings a change of mood for the sky, but not for my muscles. The clouds are gone and the blue is back. I step outside and get hit with an invisible whip of wind. After yesterday's sixty-four-miler, my legs stiffen in protest as I walk across the parking lot to check out. Kevin greets me.

"Good morning. It's gonna be a windy one."

I collapse into an armchair and watch tree branches sway, wondering what to do. Get up and go, or go curl up inside? He tells me the suite is available for another night at the same bargain rate. I feel Lillian urging me to stay, so I do.

Max and Tyler decide to push on against the wind. First they stop to check out my sweet digs. There's plenty of room for them to crash on the couch by the fake fireplace, but they're committed to camping at Conchas Lake thirty miles northwest.

I spend the day adding stickers to the bike and riding it around town. Double-wide streets with little traffic make biking a breeze, but the emptiness is haunting. Tucumcari is blessed with terrific murals yet blighted by decaying motels. Signs for the Apache, Buckaroo, Paradise, Pony Soldier, and Motel Safari are high plains hospitality artifacts from an era when cowboys and Indians were nostalgic and camels were exotic. Once vibrant colors and concepts have faded or failed. These properties are now faced with plywood or have been bulldozed into oblivion with only the motel sign marking a once profitable past. During Route 66's heyday, Tucumcari must have thrilled motorists with its drive-thru restaurants and themed motels. Now it's a textbook example of how the interstate bled Main Street dry just so we could go faster.

I retreat to the Redman Suite, turn on the heat, and dive under the covers. The thought of leaving this sanctuary makes my hands clench like clawed feet on the tub. I drift to sleep and dream what it would be like to finish my journey in Tucumcari and reopen one of these motels in the loving model of the Blue Swallow.

CHAPTER 21

WHERE DOVES CRY

Leaving Tucumcari, old Route 66 is an empty four-laner. The farther west I go, the worse it looks. Gas stations in shambles. Motels burned to the ground. A once-vibrant destination, deceased.

I rejoin I-40. Truck traffic worries me the most until I see a yellow sign warning "Dangerous Crosswinds." The next six hours I'll spend alone against the wind pounding this beige-brown sea and the blue bike that dares cross it. The sky is empty, but the wind is everywhere. It pierces my ears, stings my eyes, and poisons my mind with doubt. A weather app says it's sustained at 22 mph. These are headwinds. I can't bike. Each mile feels like a half marathon. This landscape is overwhelming and I question my presence in it. I don't know what I'm doing here anymore. This was about the experience, and I've had that. Now it feels like punishment. I've learned my lesson. New Mexico is no place for a bicycle. Now I give up. Can someone please drive me to California?

Exit 321 for Palomas is my escape from the interstate. Palomas means doves in Spanish, but I see no purity among the beer cans and soiled clothing dumped along the roadside. I cross the flyover toward an abandoned Shell station with a burned down Dairy Queen. This part of New Mexico is not in tourist brochures. Palomas is where doves cry.

My legs are crying too. My stomach is growling. Supplies are low. I'm done with pretzels and gummy bears. The last licorice pellets rattle from the Good & Plenty box into my eager hand. The valley of despair hits a few miles before Newkirk. The wind is so strong that I get off the bike and sit on the double yellow line, legs out wide and chest slumped over, hoping a car will knock me out of my misery. Alas, there is no traffic.

Newkirk only has a stamp-sized post office and a store with off-brand gas you'd only buy if the fuel light were on. I strip off my vest, jacket, gloves, and helmet before walking in. I'm in no rush. It's three o'clock. Where else can I go today moving at three miles per hour?

The store is crammed with Route 66 trinkets and packaged snacks. A man and woman stare me down. I assume they are a couple because they look like a set. In my mind I call them Mr. Bean and Billie Jean. His dark hair, big eyes, and awkward gestures remind me of the comedian Rowan Atkinson. Bean sits behind the counter looking outside like a judgy cat on a windowsill.

Billie Jean is in an office chair, armrests propping up her body. She's chewing something and watching the TV mounted above the door. She's been watching me too, and I'm peppered with questions. Where am I from? What am I doing? Why am I riding a lady's bike? She wants to trade her bike for my bike, but the only trade I'll make is for a vehicle with enough engine power to reach Santa Rosa.

I look for fresh food among the road atlases and keychains. Selection is limited to bags of chips and jerky. I'd rather gnaw on the souvenirs. Given all the candy I'm eating, you might think I'm being picky, but candy is simply energy to make the desert miles a little sweeter. Now I want real food. I press my nose against the drink cooler. I see string cheese, suspicious lunch meats, withered Clementines, and one moldy grapefruit.

Mr. Bean watches me move around his little store. I approach the counter with nothing in hand and one question in my mind.

I ask, "How far to Santa Rosa?"

"Only twenty-five miles...just down the road," he replies, turning back to a Sudoku sheet.

I already knew the answer. I'm testing his sympathy. With daylight dwindling and the wind still strong, I might make it halfway to Santa Rosa and get stuck in no man's land. Newkirk at least has Mr. Bean's store and two streets, named A and B.

"I can't make Santa Rosa," I say, pulling my helmet hair in frustration. "I've never been stuck like this. I don't know what to do."

"That's a son of a bitch," he says with a shrug, returning to his puzzle.

Why should he care? I'm the idiot riding a bike across New Mexico in November. I stand by the counter watching his pencil marks, hoping he'll come up with a solution for my problem too. The door opens and his pencil drops.

"Well, you could ask someone for a ride," he says.

I've already thought of that, but Newkirk is not the cross-roads of America.

"Maybe this trucker will give you one?"

A man with a shaved head in sweats and hoodie is cruising the snack rack. He approaches the counter where Mr. Bean diligently records purchases in his ledger. Bean then asks the man if he has room in his truck to give me a lift. My heart jolts with hope. Mr. Bean is on my side!

"Truck?" the guy cries. "Man, I ain't driving no truck. I got an '88 Chevy Caprice and the radiator is damn near busted."

The two tangle in a volley of problems and solutions. Mr. Bean suggests something, but the man isn't buying it. His voice rises against the bad advice, and he walks out to be with his ailing sedan.

Perhaps to save face, Mr. Bean tells me how much he really does know about auto repair because he's seen enough troubled cars pass through. I begin to think that maybe people break down here never to be seen again. I flash back to the early '90s flick *Nothing but Trouble* where Chevy Chase and Demi Moore are detained by a cop (John Candy) for a traffic violation in the bizarro village of Valkenvania. The cop's grandfather is a 106-year-old judge (Dan Aykroyd) with melted flesh who metes out justice from a courthouse of horrors. Despite the cast, it was a box office flop, but it terrified me as an eleven-year-old viewer. Newkirk could be a real-life Valkenvania and I need to get the hell out as soon as possible.

"Hey! Here's the weather!" shouts Jean from her chair.

We turn to the screen and I cross my fingers. Sun and wind are expected the next two days. The meteorologist circles the number fifty-seven for the day after tomorrow. That's the high for the week.

"Son of a bitch," Mr. Bean says, weighing in on the weather.

I leave the store. The Caprice is gone. I stand in fading sunlight hoping for a miracle. Two guys in a box truck ask me where I'm going, but the conversation ends after that. A pickup truck pulls in. There's room in the back, but the door says New Mexico Game Warden. That seems as hopeless as the one belonging to a state livestock brand inspector.

Here's something that could work: a pickup pulling an empty horse trailer. The driver, in a cowboy hat and boots with spurs, looks at my sweats and neon vest like I'm from Roswell. We don't speak.

Traffic tapers off with the creeping darkness. The gas station closes at seven, but reality sets in sooner. I'm not getting to Santa Rosa. I am next to the interstate, yet stuck in the wilderness. I roll my stuff to the far end of a gravel lot where truckers layover. Nobody's here now, but I wonder if I'll get dozens of wheels of company in the middle of the night.

The tent posts aren't sticking into the ground and my tarp—a thin plastic drop cloth—won't stay flat in the wind. I wedge the tent in between the detached trailer and bike, which is on its side. Headlights from the interstate beam at me on the left. Train tracks run parallel to my right. I'm hoping the cars and freight will keep the coyotes away that are howling in the dark.

I crawl inside the tent and unwrap dinner: two sticks of cheese, pretzels, and animal crackers. Thanks, Mr. Bean. My phone gets no reception and without it, I can't tether my laptop to the signal. There's nothing to do but wait until sunrise. I pull the sleeping bag tighter and burrow into the hard edge of an uneasy abyss.

CHAPTER 22

THUMBS DOWN, THUMBS UP

To Santa Fe My Way

One day and thirty miles later, I'm in Santa Rosa with no way out. Santa Rosa is a smaller and sadder version of Tucumcari with one attraction called the Blue Hole. It's a natural pool eighty-two-feet deep with water so clear you can scuba dive. I don't really care; I'm in a black hole.

Headwinds have trapped me at the Rodeway Inn and tomorrow it gets worse. I need to bike fifty-five miles with nowhere to eat or sleep along the way. Fifty-five miles. On Interstate 40. No services. No Max and Tyler. And that only gets me to Clines Corners, a glorified gas station in the desert. There's nowhere to spend the night. I need to go another full day of riding into the mountains to reach Santa Fe. Santa Rosa to Santa Fe takes two extreme days in good conditions, but the National Weather Service warns that northwest winds 25 to 35 mph will strengthen to gusts of 50. Hardcore cyclists might rise to the challenge, but I'm a commuter in old gym clothes on a bike that belongs in the

Manhattan grid, not the New Mexico desert. I've had enough of this bike and this wind. For the first time in my life, I'm going to try my hand at hitchhiking.

Days earlier Jane faced the same situation. She texted me:

Since I came into New Mexico, the wind hit me :(wasnt the wind so strong? So one day, I had to stop after going only 30 km and in Santalosa, I had to hitchhike and now Im in Alberkerki. The wind is so horrible. Where r you now?

I'm now where she was and doing the same thing: hitchhiking out of Santa Rosa. Today is Veterans Day, a holiday in name only anywhere I've worked. And yet today is the only holiday I wish I were at work. The office was an incubator of boredom, yet an anchor to routine. Out here on my own, I'm adrift with no safety net.

I skip breakfast to strategize. Santa Rosa has fewer than 3,000 people, yet it has three access points to the interstate. The female Indian motel clerk has no advice on which to target, only to say that not much traffic passes through any of them.

I borrow a marker to write "West" in bubble letters on the back of a paper from my Oklahoma hospitalization. She watches with idle curiosity, mostly to make sure that I return her marker, which is now dry after I pen a second sign for Santa Fe. I'll use that if I'm lucky enough to first get a ride to Clines Corners. That's my plan. Hitchhike west to the truck stop at Clines Corners and then find another ride going northwest to Santa Fe, where a host is ready if I make it before his bedtime at 9:00 p.m.

Now that I think about it seriously, I have no idea how to hitchhike. Do I put my thumb out, or is that like whistling for a taxi in New York? Nobody does it except in the movies. I don't think a hand gesture is enough. From my tour guiding days, I learned that if you hold a sign, people will look at it no matter what. Applying this lesson to my current situation:

Man with thumb out. Invisible.

Man with thumb and bicycle. Still invisible.

Man with thumb, bicycle, and sign. What's that sign say?

I've got a sign; now I need somewhere to stand. First I'll hit the west exit because I think locals live on that side of town. Maybe they're driving to Albuquerque for a Veterans Day sale? I lay down my gear and stand up with the sign. To look more helpless, I rest the bicycle upside-down on its seat and handlebars. Wheels point to the clear blue sky. So few cars pass that I get tired and sit on the curb. The wind blows the bike over. After an hour, I move on.

The middle exit has no room for a vehicle to stop, so I keep going to the east exit. Next to the interstate on-ramp, Phillips 66 is busy gassing up pickups and SUVs. Volume is good, but most vehicles are already packed.

A Chevy Suburban pulling a trailer leaves the gas station. California plates. California is west. Two middle-aged white women with short hair are chatting inside. Mom types. Moms love me. The back seats are empty, so there's plenty of room for a charming stranger and his bike. They look at me and the sign, waiting for cross traffic to pass before driving away. Bitches!

Can I blame them? I wouldn't stop for me either. Could be dangerous. Too much gear. But in wind strong enough to sway vehicles, I hope the bike earns me more sympathy than your average hitchhiker with a camo backpack.

A Ford Explorer makes a U-turn towards me. The back seat and trunk are empty. New Hampshire plates. *Hey ya, New*

*Hampshire. Hey! I'm hitchhiking, but I'm not crazy or a criminal.
I'm smart...graduated cum laude from Dartmouth. I spent four
years in Hanover. We have so much in common. I once had the
same license plate, Live Free or Die. I'm living free but also about
to die. New Hampshire, help!*

The wind pounds my body. It's hard work just standing out
here waiting. Another hour passes. I've tried all the exits, but
not all the gas stations at this exit. I take a final stand at Love's
truck stop. What I need is a lonely trucker. I imagine resting
my feet on the dash as we listen to Florida Georgia Line, talk
about college football or hot celebrities, and drink Bud Light,
tossing empties out the window. I'm not interested in any of
those things but imagine this is what truckers are into and why
so many cans end up on the side of the road.

My all-American trucker fantasy fizzles before I even get
to Love's. On the way, a sign warns: "Notice—Do Not Pick up
Hitch Hikers—Prison Facilities." Well, I'm not wearing orange
and nobody reads anymore, right?

I sit on the curb across from the pumps eating my lunch of
pretzels and gummy bears while holding the paper "West" on
my knee. When I'm done, I stand at the intersection that leads
into Love's. Now I'm visible to everyone on the way in and the
way out. There's no missing me. I angle my paper at oncoming
vehicles. That plants a seed. When they exit, I'll still be there
smiling through the misery.

A FedEx driver nods with amusement. I wonder if I can
package myself to his next stop. The hour passes two o'clock.
I think about my family far away. I think about the prisoners
nearby. I'm free but I'm trapped. I don't know where I'll be
tonight. Here. Santa Fe. Somewhere in between? My destiny
is to be determined at a windy truck stop in the armpit of New
Mexico.

A white pickup pulling a horse trailer slows down next to

me. The window lowers and a woman is talking. Then she gets out. The trailer is empty. In you go, Countri Bike! I climb in the back seat and we're off. My dream comes true so fast that I don't know what hits me until after it happens.

"We don't usually stop for hitchhikers," Linda explains as her husband drives me into the promised land—the on-ramp of Interstate 40.

"Actually, this is my first time, too," I admit. "Thank you so much. I was desperate. I can't bike in this wind. It's insane."

"Yup, sure blowing hard. I feel it with that empty trailer swaying in the back," says Tom, Linda's husband and my hero.

I introduce myself while overcoming the shock that my plan worked. I'm leaving Santa Rosa at 65 mph instead of three. The gentle rumble of the engine is doing the hard work, not my legs. The wind is pounding the truck, not my body.

Linda and Tom are ranchers from Texas. They're driving to California to pick up an octogenarian friend who is lonely after a bad divorce. She has no immediate family except a nephew, and they're not close. They are moving her to their horse ranch near Fort Worth and building a guest house on their property.

"She's never been to Texas," Tom says. "But she's getting worried towards the end. She doesn't want to be alone getting older. Everybody needs hope." The empty horse trailer is her moving van to a better tomorrow and mine for a better today.

"This is our around-the-ranch, two-horse trailer," Linda explains. "We used to haul a forty-footer, but we don't drive around with it empty."

Linda and Tom's business was horse hauling and their ranch once had thirty equines. Only six are left. With age, both they and the horses have moved on.

"Texas was the place to be for the horse industry," Linda sighs. "But I got so crippled up from a horse injury that I can't ride 'em no more." She now sells real estate. And Tom?

"Ah, I'm just a bum," he laughs. "I make Christmas decorations from used horseshoes. I weld them...just tack 'em together."

Linda hands me her phone to look at photos. As I praise Tom's craftsmanship, she interrupts.

"Oh look! Another biker! Well, we've already filled our quota," she laughs.

"Don't look like he's in good shape," Tom adds.

In the dirt is a guy in child's pose. He has dark skin. His bike leans on a fence post but there's no gear. Was he praying? I can't process the details because we're moving too fast. This image fragment, blurred and incomplete, is one of the most powerful of my trip. Another biker facing the same conditions. I'm saved while he surrenders to the wind on the edge of an interstate in the middle of nowhere.

I could make small talk all the way to Cali, but we are coming up on Clines Corners where a road goes north to Santa Fe. They're continuing west through Albuquerque where a train goes north to Santa Fe. Stopping in Clines Corners is faster, but I'll have to find another ride. Linda says my chances won't be good without weekend traffic. That could mean a night at a truck stop with nowhere to sleep.

The big red and yellow sign for Clines Corners appears on the horizon.

"Whadda thinking, guy?" Linda asks.

Albuquerque. It will take longer, but guarantees arrival in Santa Fe where the overnight low is twenty-six degrees. With the holiday schedule, the next train isn't for two and a half hours. The station's waiting room is closed and the temperature is falling fast with the sun. I hug Linda and Tom goodbye. He asks if I have a jacket. I lie and say that it's in my trailer. I roll my gear onto the platform where a woman is doing pushups to keep warm. I fidget in place. At least I don't need to hold a sign.

The Rail Runner to Santa Fe arrives with the state bird

painted in red and yellow on the side. Doors close with a "meep meep." The train rocks and rolls through the darkness as I drift asleep. Waking up at the Santa Fe Depot, I sense that I'm in the mountains. The darkness is a shade darker. The air is hard like an ice cube, yet sweet from burning piñon wood.

My host John doesn't live far from the station. I can't wait to get warm and cozy because I might as well be biking naked I'm that cold. My teeth won't stop chattering. Like most homes in the historic district, an adobe-style wall screens his house from the road. I knock just before nine o'clock. Based on his sleep schedule, curt emails, and lack of photo on his Warm Showers profile, I'm expecting to meet a grandpa. John is actually in his late twenties. He's a civil engineer for water resources in northern New Mexico and backs what I'm doing as "totally rad." He loves that I'm a "regular dude" on a bike share and not dressed in Spandex on a carbon fiber frame.

"People see that fancy gear and don't think it's a person underneath. It's like a soldier with armor on—doesn't look human," he says, explaining this can lead to "bike lash" from drivers who don't want to share the road with invaders on two wheels.

My ragtag threads are not insulated for November at 7,200 feet. The highest state capital in America is also one of the oldest settlements in the nation, founded before the Mayflower Pilgrims arrived.

John lends me his puffy jacket so I can run down the block to have dinner before the restaurant closes. La Choza is painted in bright colors and has wobbly furniture. The chile relleno plate with fried green chiles stuffed with Monterey jack cheese is delicious. The apple walnut cinnamon pie a la mode, drenched in fudge, is so decadent that it wipes out every negative memory of New Mexico, which has been pretty much every moment except for the Blue Swallow Motel and the ride from Linda and Tom.

The next morning John goes to work and I explore the house. John likes plants. He greeted me with a hit of weed when I came in last night. The dining room is a sanctuary for succulents like aloe, jade, and cacti. On the table is a book called *Weeds of the West* that has everything from innocent *Agavaceae* (Great Plains yucca) to awful *Zygophyllaceae* (puncturevine). Puncturevine is as sharp as it sounds and a thorn in many a cyclist's tire. It grows at the edges of roads and pastures. The bur is so sharp that it wounds livestock and kills bike tubes. Uprooting this pest isn't enough; seeds lay dormant for up to five years. This book is full of weeds that look ugly, angry, or dead, but it makes me realize that the desolate landscape I've been bitching about is in fact thriving in its own secret way.

I mosey into the kitchen. On the counter, baby herbs stretch for the window. Inside the pantry, glass jars have seeds and spices. Recipes for garam masala, chai, and cherry pie are taped inside the door. Where ya hiding the snacks, John? Just as I think about texting him, he messages that he's cooking us a vegan dinner. I'm tasked with shopping for sesame seeds, cilantro, and Rowdy Mermaid kombucha at Whole Foods. Goodbye gas station cheese. I'm back in foodie civilization.

In Santa Fe I get a little too comfortable. The bike is locked in the garage and I get around on foot. I do normal weekend things with my host like play league kickball, go to yoga, visit museums (Georgia O'Keeffe), hike in the woods with his coworkers, and watch *The Walking Dead* after a Sunday dinner party. I even go to a late-night movie with Max and Tyler who are in town. We watch the new James Bond film *Spectre*.

Santa Fe's colorful art, flavorful food, and fellow progressives push the Texas Panhandle into the dustbin of trip memories. When bone-chilling cold and five inches of snow blanket the city, I don't care. I sit by the fire inside landmark hotel La Fonda on the Plaza. Nobody knows I'm not a paying guest. I write by the crackling flames for hours. I treat John to dinner at The Shed, which won a James Beard Foundation award. I spoon up the best huevos rancheros at Tia Sophia's. Consume nachos loaded with guacamole and tongue-tickling jalapeños. Wash it down with margaritas *con sal*. I could eat my way through Santa Fe till spring. I want more of this and less of the long, empty road ahead. It's hard to get motivated, but I must move on. Albuquerque awaits and the Turquoise Trail will take me there.

I ride out of Santa Fe along paved paths with high desert brush peeking out of the snow. I start down a national scenic road called the Turquoise Trail for the next fifty miles. Everything about this part of New Mexico is quirky, earthy, and colorful. What nature doesn't make in tones of yellow, brown, and blue is painted so by artists.

The gem of the trail is Madrid, even though the tap water tastes like sulfur. Fresh water has always been a problem here. This former coal mining town boomed around the turn of the twentieth century when its population was larger than Albuquerque's. Residents enjoyed unlimited electricity and a minor league team for the Brooklyn Dodgers at the first illuminated ballfield west of the Mississippi.

After the mines closed in the 1950s, Madrid became a ghost town. The owner put the whole place up for sale at $250,000, but there were no takers. Twenty years later he a la carted each building with houses going for an average of $2,500. Most didn't have indoor plumbing, electricity, or telephone lines. The town itself had no government or public services. Yet two weeks later, every parcel was sold. The buyers, from what I read in an old article, were often in their mid-thirties. Some were artists. Others had an Ivy League degree and were on a second phase of life, determined to do something different and more meaningful. The article ends with a sculptor from Montana saying that a sense of place and belonging helped him overcome the primitive conditions. Community and identity go a long way. They can even bring a ghost town back to life and turn it into a thriving artsy enclave. I think back to Tulsa. Its downtown could use Madrid's can-do spirit to resurrect itself, maybe with my help. I even fit the profile of the changemakers from 1970s Madrid.

I bike along the main road looking for a place to stay. The buildings look Old West but have bright paint and names like Gypsy Plaza and Crystal Dragon. The vibe is funky and folksy. Shops sell jewelry, crafts, candles, and recycled art. It's made locally and by hand, often with an indigenous touch, such as turquoise stone that was first found by the Pueblo people. Nobody is out and about today. The stores are covered in shadows and the November cold makes me shiver. Camping isn't practical and Albuquerque is impossibly far. I find a room above Java Junction that sells Bad Coffee Sucks mugs in every color. I almost lose sleep overpaying one hundred dollars for the cozy upstairs apartment, but at least it includes a breakfast burrito the next morning when coffee shop aromas gently awaken me.

Rusty metal sculptures of bison heads and cowboys line the road leaving Madrid. The climb is slow and steady. I don't mind because the New Mexico of my dreams is all around me. The landscape through Tucumcari (Blue Swallow Motel) and Santa Rosa (prison facilities) was beige and unappealing. Endless straight lines fed me to the wind, which broke me down bone by bone. The scenery along the Turquoise Trail is majestic with low green brush and plateaus of red dirt. Snow-capped mountains in the distance give comfort to my powerlessness. The world feels so big as I pedal closer to the sky. I'm not going anywhere fast. I might as well be inhaling crisp mountain air rather than emissions on the interstate. I continue to climb. What goes up must come down. The payback is beautiful. I coast around curves on thrilling descents full of sunshine. I barrel downhill with the road to myself and music at full blast. I'm smiling like a dog with its head out the window of a speeding car. Saliva pools at the corners of my mouth and flies off my face.

In ABQ, the craft beer is good, but distances across town are too long on a bike. Walter White's house on *Breaking Bad* is nearly twenty miles roundtrip from where I'm staying. I skip it. Even the city's name is too long. My biggest triumph in Albuquerque is that I can now spell it, eyes closed.

My host is Bob, a man with untamed wisps of white hair and a Bernie Sanders sticker on his Subaru. Over stout beers and street tacos at Marble Brewery, Bob shares stories about American ignorance of this state. It's no secret that geography is not our national strong suit, but his examples are no joke.

Before he moved west, his physician in Virginia asked him what shots he needed to visit New Mexico. Telephone operators tried to connect him overseas. And upon presenting his New Mexico license at check-in, a hotel in Miami asked for his passport and couldn't understand how he had a US passport and a foreign driver's license.

New Mexico is an enigma and a misnomer. "Not really new, not really Mexico," sums up one bumper sticker. The Land of Enchantment is America's forty-seventh state, admitted in 1912—about four years after Oklahoma and five weeks before Arizona, the Grand Canyon State, and the next domino to fall on my way west.

CHAPTER 23

GRAND CANYON AND BIGGER TROUBLE

E arthy and woodsy, Flagstaff feels like a frontier town all alone in a national forest. Ponderosa pines sweeten the crisp air. An active railway runs alongside brick storefronts. The *clang-clang-clang* of alarm bells and low roar of locomotives make my spine tingle. I close my eyes and imagine western pioneer days of yore.

Unlike Albuquerque, Flagstaff delights me with its small scale. Cozy restaurants and microbreweries are nearby, not five miles away. When winter ends the day early, a whiskey chai warms the night inside the haunted Hotel Monte Vista.

Flag becomes my favorite stop since Tulsa thanks to a wonderful host and her friends. Samantha is an outdoor and active lifestyle photographer when not at her desk as an administrator for Northern Arizona University. She offers to drive to the Grand Canyon to get my story on video. The backdrop of a world wonder at sunrise has better lighting than her living room, she says, and I don't disagree.

In her late twenties, Samantha lives in the woods with her

new boyfriend near the Lowell Observatory, one of the oldest in the country. She tells me it was built to look for life on Mars and was where Pluto was discovered.

It's pitch black when we leave her house at 5:30 a.m. Under a starry sky we struggle to hoist the bike onto the roof rack of her jellybean coupe. The bike almost doubles the height of the car. I'm nervous it's going to break free and shatter the windshield, but Sam is focused on telling me her story as we speed through darkness to break dawn at America's grandest canyon.

The empty road is an intimate setting to talk about things that won't be recorded on film. She tells me she was married, but is now divorced from her high school sweetheart.

"He came home one day and said, 'I don't want to be married. I don't want to have a family. I don't want anyone to care about me.'"

Her world turned upside-down in minutes. The shock might have lasted forever, but she found comfort on two wheels.

"Biking gave me community. Before, I never felt like I was a part of anything. With cycling I've found a female tribe and met amazing women who are strong and powerful and are inspirational about living life," Sam says.

I nod in agreement. Cycling gave me solace from a failed relationship with myself. The bike was always there when I needed it, ready to ride wherever I wanted to go. Riding took my mind off the past because I needed to focus on the present right in front of the wheel.

First light reveals an overcast sky and empty parking lot. We set the bike near the rim's edge. I'm wearing all of my layers yet can't stop chattering as she records me talking about what I'm doing and why.

Samantha drives back to Flagstaff for work and I pedal to Bright Angel Lodge. An oversized stone hearth warms the lobby. These rustic accommodations have hosted visitors since the

1930s. Even during the off-season, a no-view cabin is a splurge, but it's my only choice. I can't sleep outside in December with lightweight camping gear.

The room isn't ready, so I go for a spin along the rim. Instinctively I head west. The rim road to Hermit's Rest is eight miles. If driving is like running in sneakers, biking is barefoot jogging on the beach. I feel a grounded connection to the Earth at the lip of what could be the planet's mouth. Even on a day when clouds mute the colors, the canyon is incredible. I can't process how deep and wide it is. Goosebumps crawl up my spine and make my head shiver.

This breathtaking detour was possible after getting a lift to the Grand Canyon. With Samantha gone, I must ride out on my own. The next morning I pedal through Ponderosa pines along a trail that takes me out of the National Park. It's sixty miles south to the town of Williams on Route 66 and I have a new toy to help me get there.

I'm about to demo the latest in bike share technology, says entrepreneur Jeff Guida who emailed me at the right time.

> Hi Jeffrey, I came across your voyage and think it is completely awesome. And I'd like to offer our help! My company, ShareRoller, has developed a small, detachable motor system that can add electric power to your Citi Bike in seconds. Perfect for when you encounter the next relentless headwind that chokes your forward progress to walking pace, or the next giant hill (or mountain!) that is just beyond the realm of possibility with a 3-speed, 45-lb Citi Bike monster.

This battery-powered motor was so innovative that Citi Bike panicked and deactivated his membership. It's only natural that two Citi Bike outlaws, both named Jeff, join forces and break the boundaries of bike sharing.

The trail ends in Tusayan where outside a grocery store I assemble ShareRoller for the first time. It's a 3D printed box for two big lithium batteries. A motorized wheel pops out like an arm to press against the front tire and move it forward. Like a tailwind giving a little push, it's designed to make biking easier so you can go farther. The invention might have taken off, but later development of electric assist built into the frame had all the benefits of ShareRoller without the hassle or heft. This thing weighs a whopping ten pounds. Cross-country cyclists obsess about shaving ounces off their load. I just added two bricks to my bag. When it's stored in the trailer, the drag is for real.

I quickly regret not testing this in advance. The battery box slides onto a metal triangle above the front wheel. But the latch on the box won't catch the anchor hole above the wheel; it's a little short. I push, I pull, I scream, I swear. My fingertips bleed from trying so hard. I call Jeff and we troubleshoot over the phone for an hour. Eventually, I MacGyver the battery box in place with rubber gear ties and pray it doesn't fall off and break.

Now it's almost noon and I've got fifty-two miles to go. I should be worried, but I'm not. With a battery-powered motor, I can pedal a modest 15 mph. Yet the device adds resistance to the front tire. This is not a kick back and relax kind of thing. Pedaling takes even more effort, kind of like riding through mud. The benefit comes when I press the throttle and the motor comes to life. I'm pedaling just as hard as before, but the motor magnifies my output. I'm going faster. Well, sometimes. It's not strong enough to push me up hills and actually slows my roll downhill. It's good only on straightaways, like cutting through commercials to return to the show.

I'd like to fast-forward these empty miles to Williams. Despite only mild use, the battery is draining fast. ShareRoller is for city streets, not for headwinds and hills while towing a trailer. The wind blows against me and I become addicted to the throttle. Without the motor, I'm hardly moving. So I throttle. Again. Just a little more. The struggle of when to stop is like deciding which chip is your last. Next thing you know, the bag is empty.

Soft pastels streak across the sky. It's beautiful yet scary. I've gone just seven miles in the last seventy-five minutes—with motorized assist. I could almost walk faster. It's 5:12 p.m. and I have six minutes until the sun sets with twenty-two miles to go and nothing out here except 20 mph headwinds. I press the throttle and the motor sputters like the last drops of soda sucked through a straw.

In Latin, *vox clamantis in deserto* means a voice crying out in the wilderness. It's the motto of Dartmouth and mentioned in the Bible. I give it a shot. Like a scorned lover, I scream at the sun to stop and turn around, but my light source slips away without apology. I strap on a headlamp and clip a red strobe to my seat pole. The motor goes in the trailer. Cinderella technology has turned into a ten-pound pumpkin.

Until now, I've been good at avoiding this danger. Along the C&O Canal, darkness stopped me as I reached Turtle Run Campground. In Tucumcari, I arrived at the Blue Swallow Motel just after nightfall. But never have I been so far from a destination at dusk.

The only way forward is State Route 64, a smooth two-lane road with fresh white paint where vehicles average more than 80 mph. Rush hour traffic—even in rural Arizona—upsets me. Tour buses leaving the Grand Canyon blow by with no clearance. Reclining passengers are nodding off on their way to somewhere safe and warm. I'm pedaling for my life on the shoulder. I begin dreaming of dinner, if I ever make it that far. I decide on smothered nachos and dark beer.

I hear another bus and look behind me. Something is off.

My light. It's gone! My flashing red taillight is dead and I have no extra batteries. I'm wearing a neon yellow safety vest over a neon yellow windbreaker. The trailer's rain cover is also yellow, so when headlights hit me I should stand out like fireworks, but otherwise I'm biking in the dark with only a faint headlamp. I scavenge reflective lane markers torn from the pavement and stick them to the trailer for added visibility.

These miles are cold and dark. Even the motivation of nachos is fading. What I want is that damn motor. Around the bend, a gas station glows like a halo. I find an outdoor outlet and spend half an hour shivering while the battery gets a little life.

I'm hoping to take the back way into Williams for the final ten miles. Leaving the gas station, Google Maps sends me onto a series of side roads that don't exist, wasting more time and energy. I can't tell where I'm going in the dark and return to the main road.

Finally entering Williams, the battery, which died again, suddenly squawks to life, surprising a group of smokers outside a bar. I stop at a few chain hotels, but they're too much for the night. My last try is the Highlander Motel, which is rather modern and comfy for forty dollars. It's now after nine and every restaurant is closing. I make it to a gastropub on Route 66 in time for those nachos, exhaling with gratitude after every chip.

Now a tourist gateway to the Grand Canyon, Williams began as a rough and rowdy town named after fur trapping frontiersman Old Bill Williams. After a rough ride of my own, I'm in no shape to leave the next morning. California can wait a day.

Despite winter's chill, I quickly warm up to Williams. Restaurants and gift shops thrive on the Route 66 business strip that is decked in ribbons and wreaths for Christmas. I'm surprised to learn the final nail in the Mother Road's coffin was hammered here. A mural on a gas station notes that on October 13, 1984, a new stretch of interstate bypassed the last downtown along Route 66.

This is no time for nostalgia. My priority is laundry. I've been wearing the same undershirt for three days, reversing it every morning. Nobody's gotten close enough to notice. In clean clothes, I explore some shops and come across Grand Canyon Brewing Company. I open the door and steam blankets me. The aroma of hops leads me deeper into the cloud. Peanut shells crunch underfoot. "Welcome to the Jungle" by Guns N' Roses is turned up to eleven. I'm in the right place, ready for wherever this goes.

The polished wooden bar with tree trunk stools is empty. I sit facing the taps like a child in front of presents on Christmas morning. A welcoming holler comes from the back. Derrick, the only server, is slapping labels on stout cylinders full of what I crave. He has close-cropped blond hair and approaches with a smile.

"You're on a bicycle—in December," he confirms with the concern of a parent while pouring me a Winter Bourbon Bomber, an easy choice given the season. "December here is kind of a roller coaster. It's unpredictable. In Williams they say that if you don't like the weather, just wait five minutes."

With snow in the forecast, the town is buzzing that it's going to look a lot like Christmas soon. But nobody knows how much or when. One to three inches tonight. Three to five all day tomorrow. Five to eight into Sunday.

"We never really know until we wake up and see it," says Ronnie whose bushy eyebrows give him a likable look even before he opens his mouth. This junior brewer just arrived and tells me about his dream of opening his own place someday. Darkness is falling and the windows are fogged up. I can't see outside and it doesn't matter. I'm embedded at the bar with Derrick and Ronnie by my side. For now, I'm safe here. Only time will tell how the flurries fall at 6,766 feet above sea level.

When I finally get up to check the conditions, I have a belly full of beer and step ankle-deep into the snow. I retreat into the steamy warmth and bury my head in my arms on the bar. This is my second night at the motel and I don't want to pay for a third.

Ronnie offers me a place to crash if the going is bad in the morning. Along with his phone number, he gives me four low-pour bottles sealed with wax. The brewery can't sell them, so they're mine. At twenty-two ounces each, I'm either going to drink them for breakfast or leave the motor behind at the motel. The beer is worth more to me at this point. Back in my room, I put wet sneakers in the bathtub to dry. I turn up the propane heater and burrow under the covers wondering what morning will bring.

I wake up coughing. My back is sweaty, my mouth is dry, and my head hurts. Why did I drink so much last night? Daylight peeks around the edge of the closed curtains. I stumble out of bed and tear them open. White light floods the room, blowing me back into bed as I shield my eyes. It's horrible. Everything is white. I can't even see the black asphalt. My fingers tremble as I text for help. Ronnie's already at the brewery and tells me to come over. It's still coming down as I push the bike through the powder, thinking this could be the end of my ride. Even more snow is in the forecast.

I've got nowhere to go and nothing to do except finish those four big bottles. The brewery becomes home for the day. I sit at the bar with my laptop and give the guys a hand moving stuff around, literally getting my feet wet as hoppy steam coats my skin. The master brewer gives me a tour. He explains the fermentation process, tank capacities, and technical details that I quickly forget, but it's fun to feel part of this place, walking around the back-of-house with a beer in my hand like I belong here. This camaraderie, although temporary, nourishes my growing loneliness across the Southwest.

Ronnie invites me to join his friends for dinner. We share dessert and keep the night going at the "world famous" dive bar Sultana. A stuffed mountain lion above the bar looks ready to pounce. Other animal heads watch the action at pool tables. The place has an Old Western vibe and feels like it's been around forever. More than one hundred years, says the bartender, adding that the town's first police chief was shot and killed outside the bar. Yes, I imagine a wrong look here could escalate into broken pool cues and a body going through the plate glass window. I'm not worried. I'm living the dream of an adult snow day in a small town whose brewery and staff are my home and family for two nights. Let it snow. I'll deal with reality in the morning.

CHAPTER 24

A GERMAN, A BARBER, AND A GUN FANATIC

The roads are clear, but another round of snow is coming tomorrow. My window to escape the high altitude is now or never. I leave Williams with a fully charged ShareRoller but won't need it due to an epic downhill on my way to Seligman forty-two miles away. The only bad news is that Route 66 disappears for a while and I'm forced back onto the interstate.

A green highway sign with a shield for I-40 points to Los Angeles. I stop and stare. It's the first time seeing the name of my final destination, which according to the next green sign is still 458 miles away. The shoulder is wide and clear of snow, giving me confidence at what is strangely becoming second nature—pedaling a bicycle next to semis going seventy.

At first, I climb. The long hill drains my energy. I expect gravity to be doing the work, but I'm pedaling against it. Where's this downhill? I want it. I need it. I demand it. Ahead, yellow signs warn truckers to test their brakes. I'm cresting like a roller coaster before it plunges.

The shift is on. I hold my breath. I'm going so fast that icy headwinds give me brain freeze. For six miles my legs don't move. That distance normally takes an hour of effort, but I am in bike-gone-wild mode. Thanks to a gift from the topography gods, I barrel ahead with raw confidence. I feel like I'm in a video game with a magic forcefield and fast-paced music letting all the other characters know I'm invincible, so watch out. I slalom through a minefield of exploded tire treads and ice chunks blown off trucks driving alongside me. I can't lose.

After the terrain flattens, I exit the highway. I follow a lonely stretch of Route 66 that goes so far into the distance it could be California on the horizon. It's not. Hours later I arrive in Seligman ready to play the what's-your-rate game with any motel that doesn't look like a meth lab incubator.

Lodging here is a question mark because a town ordinance prohibits chains, says Klaus. He owns a motel where each cinder block room has a theme. I get Elvis. He explains that Seligman is franchise-free thanks to the efforts of an activist who is also the oldest active barber in the country. Born in 1927, Angel Delgadillo still rides a bike a few blocks to work. Angel is best known as the guardian angel of Route 66. He and other business owners banded together after the interstate bypassed Seligman in 1978. Angel led the charge to put his little town back on the tourist map, starting with wayfinding signage for what became the road less traveled as soon as the interstate opened.

"People come from Siberia to Seligman, and when they check in, the first thing they ask is, 'Where is Angel the barber?'" Klaus says in accented English.

Klaus is German. He came as a tourist in the '80s and never left. He lived for a few years in the Pacific Northwest with a home on the ocean, but decided it was too rainy and moved to California. On a road trip to Arizona he stayed at this motel. When he woke up, he saw the place was for sale and bought it.

"Millions of tourists pass through here every year going

to the Grand Canyon and seeing Route 66," he says, adding that the quality of life is great with no crime and one German restaurant. Seligman is actually named after a German railroad financier. More recently it was the inspiration for the fake town of Radiator Springs in the animated movie *Cars*, although others stake claim to the Pixar movie, such as Adrian, Texas, where I slept on the floor with Max and Tyler.

Vintage cars rust outside local businesses. The main drag looks like a 1950s time warp without ugly plastic signs for Motel 6, McDonald's, and Family Dollar. Home-grown alternatives include the Roadkill Cafe, my first choice for dinner had the stern German not made a stink about how bad it was.

Souvenir shops are full of Route 66 merchandise, made in China, of course. The irony is that many Chinese come all the way to this authentic town to buy trinkets mass produced over there. Nevertheless, the Rusty Bolt and Historic Seligman Sundries are run by Route 66 diehards who reminisce about the glory days and dream of revival. I've spent so much time on this road that no souvenir is needed. I pause at a vintage police car in the parking lot and feel uneasy as an icy wind tears down the empty street.

The next morning I'm packed and ready to go. I open the Elvis curtains and see a landscape frozen in place. The snow isn't deep, but the roads aren't clear. I should have come in the summer. Thirty tour buses a day stop here so the Chinese and Europeans can get their kicks on Route 66. That's what Billy tells me. He's a merchandise clerk who pulls double duty as the cook in winter.

"I love to mix things up in the kitchen," he says while taking my lunch order.

I'm stranded for another snow day, but there's no brewery in

Seligman. The best I can do is hang out at a gift emporium cafe with Billy, a self-described "redneck with a creativity problem." A hard worker in all seasons, Billy, for the first time in four years, is going on vacation next month.

"Going somewhere warm, I hope? Mexico's not far. I could almost bike there," I laugh.

"Nah, I'm going home, shuttin' the door and sit in my recliner. And if I get bored I'll go ta the shootin' range across the street and shoot some stuff up," he says and then rattles off gun names and parts until I can't take it anymore.

"Dude, I'm from New York City!" I cry. "We don't have guns. I have no idea what you're talking about!"

"You liberal pussies," he laughs and starts yapping about a waterproof rifle he made. "I also keep a .22 under my pillow and got a .25 ACP stashed in my boot. I'm loaded! I'm ready for the apocalypse!"

Billy reaches down to his boot. My eyes widen in fear of getting a firearm pushed in my face. Instead, he brandishes a switchblade and Leatherman survival tool.

"I'm loaded!" he screams again. "If those terrorists come here, I'm shootin' back. This ain't fucking France," he cries, referencing the Bataclan massacre in Paris that killed 130 concertgoers a few weeks earlier.

Billy tells me he ran away with the circus in seventh grade. He stayed for sixteen years before falling out in Phoenix. At a keg party he met a fellow motorbiker who persuaded him to be his roommate and ended up "adopting" him. Billy keeps referring to him as "daddy." A mutual passion for building motorcycles and shooting guns brought the men together. They looked at a map of Arizona, closed their eyes, and a finger landed on Seligman. So here they are. I would have tried again, peeking just enough to land on Flagstaff or even Williams to live behind Grand Canyon Brewing Company.

Despite ranting about violence, Billy has kind eyes and a young face that narrows into a long goatee. A ponytail flows from the back of his baseball hat. I'm putting together the pieces of his personal history and filling in gaps with my imagination. I think Billy could be coupled as a gay redneck with gun-toting machismo to overcompensate. Before curiosity gets the best of me, I shut up and stop asking questions. I'm hoping to eat in peace, but Billy's got one more thing to share. Rattlesnake eggs.

"You'n ever seen'em?" he asks with a crooked smile.

I say I haven't seen the eggs or their parents and would like to keep it that way, but Billy comes over holding a yellow envelope with a snake's mouth printed on it. As I peer inside it rattles to life. I shriek and recoil, knocking into the table as my drink tumbles to the floor. I just fell for a cheap prank made with a rubber band and paper clip. Billy howls with delight. He careens around the store with arms out like airplane wings as if scoring the winning goal at the World Cup. Arizona Rednecks 1, Liberal City Suckers 0.

The store is closing in an hour, maybe sooner because nobody's here except me and I'm leaving. The heat is off and my toes are cold, so I take food back to the room to eat with Elvis. I dial up the thermostat, get under the covers, open my laptop, and begin to write about a snow day in Seligman, population 456.

The sun has melted the snow on the road, but the blue sky is deceptive. You can't see the cold. I'm bundled up, ready to leave Seligman and begin the longest uninterrupted stretch of Route 66. It's easy to see why—there was never anything here to interrupt. Even the interstate, which replaced 66, bends away in magnetic opposition.

The next twenty-five miles are flat and barren except for

the occasional ranch house in the distance. There are no cars, just me moving slowly through beige fields speckled with white clumps of snow. When a horn blasts, I almost fall off the bike. Is the Mother Road playing tricks on me? An orange and black BNSF freight train appears, the engine's roar fighting against the cold. I've entered a Salvador Dalí fantasy where place and space don't matter. A train parallels my path in the middle of nowhere. Even the perfect blue sky and white puffy clouds look surreal. Random thoughts swirl around my mind like abstract shapes on a Kandinsky canvas.

I'm not tripping, but the temperature is getting to me. The headwinds are so icy that it feels like I'm biking in my underwear. I never imagined that testicles could turn into ice cubes, but I fear the family jewels are freezing over. I stuff cold hands down my pants to feel what's going on. I need more protection. I rummage through the trailer to pull out mesh shorts and nylon cargo pants. I'll wear these on top of thin sweatpants and synthetic boxer briefs. Not your ideal winter attire, but I packed in August never thinking I'd get as far as Arizona or December. Four layers around my waist is just good enough.

Now for my fingers, which are in pin-pricking pain. My bike gloves have exposed fingertips, so I put two pairs of ankle socks on my hands. I can still grip the handlebars, but the thin fabric is useless. I keep going, but have to stop again from the pain. The biting wind also chews through my mesh running shoes and three pairs of cotton socks. My over-layered feet are sweating, and when that hot moisture turns cold, my toes go numb.

I stop and scream. At the invisible wind. At this stupid road to nowhere. At the empty miles ahead. At summer's warmth gone cold. I've reached the point where hell has in fact frozen over. I tear at my shoelaces and rip off my sneakers. I peel away three pairs of damp socks and stand barefoot on Mother Road herself.

"WORK, GODDAMMIT, WORK!"

I'm hopping up and down, trying to feel pain and yelling at my feet to wake up and do their job. Pedal me to someplace warm. I turn the socks inside out and put them back on, apologizing to the imaginary motorists stopped behind me. I loosen the laces for better blood flow, but it's too late. A few miles later I'm walking up a hill and feel strangely disconnected from the ground. My entire feet are numb.

On the downhill side is the entrance to Grand Canyon Caverns, the largest dry caverns in the United States. Dry and underground sounds good right about now. The two-lane road widens to a four-lane divided highway, the first in Arizona. Traffic once bottled in both directions, so turn lanes had to be added near the entrance. The extra capacity seems laughable today. I'm the only one on the road and in the parking lot.

Above the caves is a compound with a motel, restaurant, convenience store, and campground. The current owners bought the land for $1.5 million, which they made back in a little more than a year. You'd never know the place is profitable just by looking at it.

The motel lobby is deserted. A clerk, who like the train appears out of nowhere, tells me it's eighty dollars for the night. "US dollars?" I ask. I'd rather risk loss of both feet and pedal eleven miles to find lodging on the Hualapai Tribe's reservation.

I weigh the options while defrosting in the Betty Boop breakfast room. My wallet thaws first when the clerk offers sixty. I'll use the savings to take a cavern tour, which I guess is obligatory for anyone stuck here overnight. I don't care so much about geology as I do the temperature. Twenty-one stories underground, the caverns are a constant sixty degrees. That's forty degrees warmer than on Earth's surface right now. I've never been so happy at sixty degrees and zero humidity. My clothes dry quickly and I regain feeling in my feet. I don't want the tour to end. Could I spend the night down here? As a matter of fact, yes.

I learn the caverns are the world's deepest underground hotel room, priced at $800 per night. The deal breaker isn't the cost, but the hideous duvet that is the same as on my sixty-dollar bed. Also, there's no plumbing. The toilet "flushes" only a few times, so Gilbert the tour guide says to make each one count. He also explains that after the Cuban Missile Crisis, JFK ordered the caverns to be turned into a bomb shelter. Enough food and water were squirreled away to sustain 2,000 people for two weeks.

It's not The Ritz-Carlton, or even Klaus's themed motel, but our guide says supplies were recently refreshed. Pallets of new bottled water were carried down one box at a time over three weeks of twelve-hour days. The six rolls of toilet paper are also new, but the emergency crackers, carbohydrate supplements, and hard lemon candies are 1960s originals.

Gilbert moves on to stalactites, but I interrupt. Did he say six rolls for 2,000 people? Not to worry, he assures. Those cardboard crackers will plug everyone up pretty good. Apocalypse note to self: bring two-ply and snacks. Actually, in the event of thermonuclear war, toilet paper wouldn't be your first concern. Getting here would, and I don't recommend a bicycle.

Back in my cinder block room, I stare at the ugly bedspread, mismatched furniture, and ancient television, which might predate the cave's formation sixty-five million years ago. The lighting makes me feel sick. I'm chilly. The clerk warned me not to use the window unit for heat because it just sucks in cold air. The only source of warmth is a bathroom heater the size and power of a toaster. I decide to camp indoors. I insert the sleeping bag under the covers and dream of tomorrow's downhill ride to warmer temps in Kingman, one city closer to Cali.

Part Four

CALIFORNIA AND BEYOND

"The world breaks everyone and afterward many are strong at the broken places."

—ERNEST HEMINGWAY, *A FAREWELL TO ARMS*

CHAPTER 25

CALIFORNIA DREAMIN' AND REALITY BITES

Maybe it's the double-wide streets with no traffic or the beige mountains against deep blue skies, but Kingman kinda wins me over. I like a frontier feel, and this town's got just that. The *Daily Miner* is the local paper. Ranching and gold mining groomed Kingman to be the seat of Mohave County, Arizona.

Kingman is the end of Route 66, at least for me. California is close, but I can't go on. Farther west on 66, the places on the map aren't more than a gas station or ghost town. Between Needles and Barstow, there are about 170 miles with no water or shelter. I get fifty miles per day at best. There's no way I can make it four days in the Mojave Desert.

Instead, I drop south and follow the Colorado River that separates Arizona and California. I take refuge in snowbird colonies around Lake Havasu. Palm trees surround a truck stop like an oasis. I refill my water bottle and strip down to two layers, a nice change from one hundred miles ago when I was in four pairs of pants and five pairs of socks (three on my feet, two on my hands). I continue along smooth asphalt and begin a sweeping downhill to a lake as big as the sea. The sun falls behind the mountains with an orange and purple sky leading to California.

"Lake Havasu!" I scream, making my arrival official. I never heard of this place until a few days ago, yet here I am wide-eyed and happy. That's the beauty of this ride—making memories across an America I never knew existed.

After two nights, I leave Lake Havasu City. I bike deeper into the river valley with naked rock walls. I'm focused on the two-lane road ahead, but glimpses of opaque turquoise water make my skin tingle. I feel like I'm in the Middle East, maybe Jordan or Oman. A caravan of camels led by Bedouin in head-cloths and white tunics could be around the next curve. Then RV parks come into view. What better contrast to America's natural beauty than bloated vehicles with mismatched plastic furniture outside.

Lake Havasu City leads to Parker and Parker leads to my fifty-mile exit from Arizona. Irrigation canals box in green fields. The land is flat and boredom is the biggest challenge. To count down to California, I eat one Skittle at every mile marker. That takes too long, so I double the reward before giving in and emptying the bag onto my taste buds screaming for more sugar.

The sky is on fire when I cross the Colorado River on a pedestrian bridge next to Interstate 10. Suddenly I'm in California. Sunny California. Beautiful California. Blythe, California? There are many exciting parts of the Golden State. Blythe isn't one of them.

Fortunately, one of its 20,000 residents is a Warm Showers host. The address is a bait and tackle shop on a rural agricultural road. I don't know if I'm gonna sleep with worms and fishies and I don't care. I'm ready to celebrate my arrival in California—2,741 miles since a nervous start on August 7. Christmas is on Friday.

Ever show up to a party and not know anyone—even the person who invited you? That's how I feel standing in a parking lot of pickup trucks wondering what to do.

"Well, hello, you must be Jeff. We've been waiting for you!" claps Dedee, the store manager I've been emailing to coordinate camping. Her bobbed hair, round cheeks, and sweet voice put me at ease. She leads me into the side yard where silhouettes gather around a fire in an oil drum. The conversation breaks and Dedee introduces me to the townie couples in their fifties and sixties. The first question is which way I'm going.

"I biked *from* New York," I say with lip-smacking satisfaction now that I'm in my final state, although just six miles deep.

"Damn, someone get this guy a beer!"

Another man hollers in agreement and I'm handed a can of Coors. From the digital jukebox Frank Sinatra sings, *Start spreading the news, I'm leaving today.* I guess New Yorkers are a novelty in this part of Cali. With Ol' Blue Eyes crooning in the background, people volunteer memories of the Big Apple, some of which predate the song.

"Oh, honey, it's been a million years," a woman tells her husband as the weight of nostalgia pushes her head onto his shoulder. "Now, we were last there in '64 or '65...when the World's Fair was there."

That was fifteen years before I was born. "Sounds like time for a refresher! I'm a licensed tour guide. And I have a travel app all about the city," I chime, handing her a business card. With this ride almost over, I need to think about restarting my revenue stream.

"I just seen it in the movies," a man says. "And that's good enough for me."

His wife agrees, "I couldn't do New York, but I like Seattle. I don't like LA...LA is too expensive. And San Francisco, my gosh, San Francisco has gotten very expensive."

"I like San Diego," says another. "Weather's perfect and it's never cold."

"San Diego? Too many people, not enough dirt," barks Bob, who is happy right here in the Colorado Desert. He's an outdoorsy type who likes camping, fly fishing, and Marlboros. His hunter green vest and denim jeans are weathered like his voice.

"I was born and raised in Minnesota an' lived most my life in the mountains of Idaho and Montana, so I know cold," he says, kicking his boot into the ground. "It'll never be as cold there as in the desert here. Colder than Colorado. Colder than Montana. Colder than Idaho. Ah hell, colder than a nude nun in a tin boat."

SoCal so cold? Nice story, Bob, but I'm not buying it.

"I know cold," he says sternly, ending the conversation.

I look away to the fire. Another log is dropped and the flames rejoice. Campfires are warm—not just with heat, but also with the bonds they kindle. I inhale the smoky scent of belonging and gaze at the stars. Meeting new people in new places is worth the long hours of riding alone.

"We're in for some severe weather, my friend. You geared up?" Bob asks, crashing my thoughts back down to Earth.

Oh Bob, c'mon. I'm thinking, enough with the scary stories. I'm 200 miles and change from Los Angeles; what's the worst that can happen? Walk the rest of the way?

"Well, I packed for my trip in August," I laugh, letting loose a hiccup. I recount not-funny-at-the-time stories from Arizona when I put socks on my hands as gloves. "And I'm done with that!" I shout, cracking open a new can for emphasis. I smile and gulp some beer. "Palm trees all the way to LA, right? I mean, this is SoCal—land of sunshine and citrus. Isn't there a law it has to be warm?"

The group is silent. My confidence has gone too far.

"You're in the desert, son," Bob growls. "I seen a lotta other bikers and you're geared a little different."

I don't respond. The group resumes chatting without me and I pick up on the word "wind." I put down the beer and reach for my phone. The glow hurts my eyes as I adjust to what I'm reading. My hand trembles. This can't be right. The overnight low is near freezing and a National Weather Service warning kills my buzz.

*AFFECTED AREA...Southeast California and Far Western Arizona...including cities of Yuma, Blythe, Parker, and Quartzsite.

*WINDS...North winds 30 to 35 mph with gusts to 45 mph.

*IMPACTS...Motorists on east-west oriented roadways such as I-10 will encounter hazardous crosswinds that can make driving difficult. Blowing dust will cause rapid reductions in visibility.

Bob moves closer. I brace for another scolding. "The wind shear here is really something," he says. "Trucks on the interstate carrying mobile homes and, poof, the homes are gone. They can't even find 'em."

That sounds like Wizard of Oz weather. Riding a bicycle next to high profile vehicles through swirling sand? I'll end up flattened like the Wicked Witch of the East. I tell Bob that I might be staying in Blythe longer than one night. He says that bikers camp in the backyard, but because of the weather, he offers me his fifth wheel. My once glowing New York swagger is reduced to ashes. First, I don't know anything about the local climate and now more embarrassment.

"Umm...what's a fifth wheel?" I ask, hoping I'm not getting into some weird couples thing.

Before Bob answers, Dedee bursts in like sunshine. "Oh,

you're so lucky, he doesn't let just anyone in there. We call it Bob's Marriott!"

I follow Bob into the dark backyard. Leaves crunch with every slow step. I can't see where I'm going and don't know what I'm getting into. Is *Fifth Wheel Marriott* Cali slang for love hotel?

Parked alongside an irrigation canal is a camper trailer. Now I get it. A fifth wheel gets towed by a pickup truck. The trailer hasn't been used in months, maybe years. Bob puts a little flashlight in his mouth and fishes for wires, plugging one into the power pedestal.

"The heat don't work, but it's got electric," he says, slapping his hand on the dusty trailer. "And no water, but you can shower in the house."

The inside is bare except for a mattress in the sleeping den. I'm not sure who or what last lay there, but I'll make it work. I'm just grateful not to be camping.

Dedee invites me into the store for dinner—ham, brussels sprouts, and mac and cheese her husband made for her. She saved me some and says to take any chips and drink I want from the shelves. Moments later, her cursing draws me over. It's the microwave. None of the number buttons are working.

"Ah heck," Dedee pouts. "Well, I just put everything on POP-CORN and it turns out OK." We both laugh. That's my strategy, too. Warm food is warm food.

As the microwave whirls, I browse kitschy signs like "Big mouth in charge" and "Men are like fish. They always get in trouble when they open their mouth." The most clever is their own bumper sticker that reads "B&B Tackle. Where all the Masterbaiters Come."

A man walks in to buy some cigarettes. I recognize him from around the fire. He hasn't said anything, but apparently my stories from freezing cold Arizona made an impression. He buys me the last B&B hoodie, an XXL that's three sizes too big. This sweatshirt is a warm gesture that becomes my fondest memory of Blythe.

Outside, the fire is dying and people are leaving. I retreat to Bob's Marriott. I'll spend the next four nights here alone, including Christmas Eve and Christmas Day.

High winds amplify the holiday solitude, yet I find comfort in the words of Bob himself, "This is a sanctuary, brother. Lots of good people. You're a long way from New York and you're always welcome out here."

As daylight streaks over the Marriott, a duck quacks me awake. The trailer is not shaking anymore. The wind is gone and so am I. After a late start, I delay further for an early lunch. Rebel BBQ's smoked brisket sandwich with jalapeño potato salad is the only food I can count on for the rest of the day. It's some of the best BBQ I've had all trip, making indulgence now worth the risk of running out of daylight later.

Euphoria over biking in California ends at the ghostly Blythe Airport. After nine miles on back roads, I'm forced onto the interstate for the next forty. No other road cuts through the desert at this latitude.

I merge onto the shoulder heading toward LA. So is everyone else. Christmas was on Friday and today is Sunday. After a few nervous miles, the constant rush of traffic becomes white noise and I focus on the unending ribbon of asphalt ahead. I use the motor lightly. The open desert and distant mountains cast a calming spell. I move at a slow pace and even heartbeat. Minutes melt into hours.

Tens of thousands of vehicles pass, but all it takes is one to ruin my day or life. From a benign Prius with a distracted driver to a pickup truck with antler side mirrors and monster tires, any vehicle is potentially dangerous. Add to the list: asshole RV. You don't need a special license to operate one of these rolling villas. You also don't need a special license to be an asshole.

By the time I hear *blump-rump blump-rump blump-rump* of tires on rumble strips, it's too late to look into my helmet mirror. The threat isn't behind me—it's next to me. The RV is so close that I can touch it. So close that I don't have time to freak out. This can't be by accident. This asshole is trying to run me off the shoulder. Do I stand my ground and risk getting crushed, or eject off the bike and crash?

Frozen with fear, I hold steady and so does he. The slang term, I learn later, is "skimming," or driving as close as possible to a bicycle without hitting it. It's a fine line between that and vehicular manslaughter. After skimming me, the RV muscles back into traffic.

As the shock wears off, my outrage begins to boil. I'm mad as hell, but what can I do, speed up and cut him off? I didn't even catch the license plate state. The RV is a one-time threat compared to cracks in the shoulder that jolt the bike every ten feet. Even worse, the edges are jagged and could tear my tires, especially the thinner ones on the trailer. As a bonus handicap, all that Christmas wind blew sand onto the shoulder, creating mini dunes that force me to stop and walk.

I'm making poor time and will run out of daylight before Desert Center. There's no food or lodging, just a golf course and housing development. I plan to charm my way inside a Riverside County fire station and join the guys for chili and garlic bread.

Fading sunlight hangs above the Red Cloud Mountains, which are living up to their name. I've biked in the dark, but never on an interstate in the dark. This is the craziest thing I've done since putting the bike on a boat to New Jersey. I take the next exit off I-10 to prepare for nightfall. No structure is any-where in sight. This is literally an exit to nowhere. As I consider wild camping, I gobble the leftover potato salad and watch the sunset, wishing I could catch up to those last rays.

I check Google Maps for another way west. It doesn't sound promising, but I pedal toward Gas Line Road. Before I reach it, the pavement ends and Bureau of Land Management signs warn motorists to have plenty of oil and gas for the sandy road ahead. In the distance, a cloud of dust billows behind oncoming headlights in the creeping darkness. Bandidos. Drug runners. That scene from *Deliverance*. I don't wanna be out here alone. I turn around and pedal hard.

A white pickup truck with tinted windows and monster tires is gaining on me. I pull over hoping it leaves me alone, but it stops and the window rolls down. Expecting to see the barrel of a gun, I am instead greeted by a concerned father.

I ask him about back roads to Desert Center. He shakes his head, confirming that I'm screwed. He's headed west to Orange County and offers me a lift. I share the back seat with his teen-age son and friend who are dozing after a day of off-roading.

The vibration of the engine massages my tailbone. Thin orange lights on the console are hypnotizing. Half of me wants to stay seated and end this journey tonight, but the other half asks to be left in Desert Center. The dad advises against it and takes the following exit for Chiriaco Summit, which at least has a coffee shop. Not much has changed since Joe Chiriaco opened a gas station and general store in 1933 with one dollar in a cigar box till. His timing was good. That same day a paved road opened in front of his property.

About ten years later, General George S. Patton founded the Desert Training Center. As its first commander, Patton liked how this harsh landscape resembled North Africa where he would lead 35,000 men into Morocco. More than a million recruits trained here to fight in World War II. A museum and memorial to Patton now stand on the grounds.

We drive behind the building and find a sandy lot with retired tanks rusting in peace. The bouncing tires wake the kiddos who *ooh* and *aah*. This is where I will camp, right out of a Boy Scout fantasy. Even dad is excited as he helps offload Countri Bike. These camo-painted tanks are even bigger than his truck. But with temps dropping to the thirties, camping in the General's backyard is less thrilling to me. If they want to spend the night, I'll trade my tent and bike for the keys to Orange County.

They drive away, leaving me alone next to tank treads. The muzzle points to the coffee shop where I'll sit until closing to recharge my devices and keep warm. Tonight is a drill for a bigger battlefield. My reward for roughing it in a war machines graveyard will be to awake in position to enter Joshua Tree National Park, and I won't need the interstate to get there. In fact, I'm done with biking on interstates forever. Where's my can of Coors? But now is not the time to celebrate.

The next two days will be off the grid. I'm not going to North Africa, but I am entering a wilderness four times the size of New York City with no source of food, water, electricity, heat, or cell service. By comparison, I'd give Bob's Marriott five stars.

CHAPTER 26

NIGHTMARE AT JOSHUA TREE

Where Two Deserts Become One

General Patton is remembered for his winning field strategies. Some of that genius must have rubbed off on me camping next to his tanks. Rather than head west toward Indio on the interstate, I'll avoid it and cut north through Joshua Tree National Park.

I wanna get off I-10 where I've battled cracked pavement and asshole RVs. Instead, I'll explore a Dr. Seuss landscape with smooth boulders and spindly Joshua trees where the Mojave and Colorado collide into one desert with an altitude problem. This place surpasses 5,000 feet above sea level. J-Tree is high and wide. At 1,250 square miles, it's larger than Rhode Island and four times the landmass of NYC—without a single Duane Reade pharmacy to buy overpriced snacks.

Built like a tank for the streets of New York, my forty-five-pound bike is way out of its element. And so am I. Joshua Tree is home to fierce winds, cryptobiotic crusts, active fault lines, hairy tarantulas, five-inch scorpions, honeypot ants, kangaroo rats, and twenty-five kinds of serpent—all of which sound terrifying to a city mouse like me.

I enter the park from the south. Cottonwood Campground is only seven miles away, but it's uphill. All uphill. The road twists and turns through rocky mounds that block the horizon, but never once bends down in relief. Even when I'm sure the top is around the next corner, there's one more hill to go. SUVs with California and Nevada plates speed by. The road is narrow and sand licks the edge. This is a National Park, not a pipeline to Vegas, so I'm hoping drivers are in a forgiving mood upon seeing a bicycle fight gravity. One family stops to give me fruit.

Two hours later I reach Cottonwood Visitor Center, the southern gateway to the park. I buy a multi-day pass for ten dollars and question why I'm paying the same rate as a motorcycle. The ranger looks at me like it's my own damn fault for not having a motor, which actually I do, but it's useless on these hills and sits in the trailer as dead weight.

As I pedal the last mile to the campground, a silver Prius pulls over. Out pops my fraternity brother Ben whom I know better by his house name, Hoser. I haven't seen him or his now-wife Jenn in ten years. They met playing beer pong in our smoky frat basement and are now living more soberly in San Diego. Jenn is an associate at a national law firm. Ben is an English and lit teacher at a private school, quite a turnaround from how I remember him at Dartmouth—incoherently drunk at four in the afternoon or passed out on the chapter room couch that he'll wet in his sleep, hence the nickname.

Our reunion isn't random. Over Facebook we coordinated to meet near Cottonwood on their way home to San Diego, but without cell service today I wasn't sure where or when. Luckily, rangers told them where the guy on the blue bike was going. They had planned to camp here over Christmas, but with temps in the twenties and winds in the fifties, retreated to a motel. They give me bananas, oranges, and leftover shortbread Christmas cookies. Eager for a little company, I ask about adopting one of their funny-faced Shih tzus, but the dogs stay in the car. We hug each other goodbye and promise to keep in touch.

Sandy patches between desert shrubs are good enough to plant a tent. The campsite is basic, but it's blessed with drinking water and flush toilets. Those are luxury amenities around here. This is the last chance for either until I leave the park in two days.

Amazingly, I'm not the only biker. Cynthia, an adventure guide, and Bob, a forest firefighter, flew their bikes from Alaska to San Diego. Joshua Tree has been a shock to the outdoorsy couple, who I imagine pal around with moose on the tundra in their spare time. At Jumbo Rocks, where more than one hundred campsites are packed together, they said it was hard to find peace.

"I've never shared a wilderness experience with that many people," says Bob. "In the morning, three women in slippers walked through my tent site. I mean, I hadn't even had coffee and they're already violating my space...in fuzzy slippers!"

Our bikes draw the attention of Peter, who is cycling alone, and like Bob and Cynthia came in from the north entrance. He's an electrician at LAX and rides his bike sixteen miles to work. By leaving his equipment truck parked at the airport, he saves $140 a week in gas. He says the only problem is cabs crashing into him on the departures level.

We disperse to set up camp before dark. I'm at a picnic table knifing peanut butter out of the jar and into my mouth when Peter comes over with an important discovery. Leftover firewood. When sleeping outside at 3,000 feet in December, finding firewood is like winning Powerball of the high desert.

After the sun goes down, Peter sparks a flame without a

match. Team Alaska comes over for more conversation as granules of snow pelt our clothing. A desert mouse with a long tail scurries by Cynthia's foot hoping to sneak into our warming party. By seven fifteen, only embers are left and we call it a night. It's pitch black and there's nothing to do without light, warmth, or cell reception.

I wake up with neck pain and frozen toes at five o'clock, thrilled at how "late" it is. Only two more hours of misery until I feel the sun. At first light I emerge and see a dusting of snow and ice on the tent. Peter's up and comes over to say goodbye. We talk about our routes. He's going south to the Salton Sea. All downhill for him. I'm going north on the hardest part of the entire trip. No source of food, water, or shelter. No electricity or cell service. No easy way out. No easy way up. I'll gain 1,700 feet over nine miles from Cholla Cactus Garden to Belle Campground where I'll spend the night.

Before my day gets harder, Peter says I'll get to relax. "Yeah man, you won't need to pedal for a while," he smiles, tracing his finger on the map over the long downhill into Turkey Flats. "Then it's pretty flat to Ocotillo Patch, but by Cholla Garden you start climbing and then you'll give it all back and then some up to Belle. It's a real climb."

Leaving the campground I'm alone again, but with each curve I get closer to the dreamy downhill that Peter promised. When the flat washes come into view, a lump forms in my throat. The valley floor is endless. One hundred New Yorks could fit here, maybe a thousand. My eyes scan the horizon to find something familiar. I keep looking, but there is no sign of human development other than this road. I'm having another Grand Canyon moment, but this time I'm going into the canyon. The pavement is flying under me. I'm falling with gravity yet soaring with emotion. My jaw drops and I gulp dry air with my eyes and mouth wide open.

From behind, a car creeps next to me and it's getting too close. I flash back to the RV that tried to run me off the road. I brake to let the car pass, but the window rolls down and an Asian woman in broken English asks if I work for the park. She's looking for directions to the north exit. This is the only road through the park and, yeah, we're heading north.

If she were looking for Joshua trees I'd be more sympathetic. I haven't seen any of the park's telltale flora, which means I'm not getting my ten dollars' worth. Instead, I obsess over the teddy bear cholla. The name is cute and the cactus looks soft, but this prickly thing leaves you writhing in pain if you dare cuddle it. Hoser, ever the fool, put his palm on one, "just to see," and shared these words of wisdom: "Stay the fuck away from the cholla!"

I admire with eyes only. To pass time, I wink when I see one. Left eye if the cholla is on the left side and right eye if on the right. This is how I pass time while riding a bicycle across a double desert. At Cholla Cactus Garden I stop the winking game because my eyelids are fluttering. A car pulls into the parking lot. The driver and passenger look at me like I'm a mirage. Reed and Lucy live on the Upper East Side. We chat about my journey, which is a nice delay to what's ahead.

From Cholla Garden to Belle Campground is nine miles uphill. Curves wind out of sight. The climb is too much even in the lowest gear. I walk and push, taking breaks to read every informational sign. I'm going to be the world expert on Joshua Tree if I ever make it out of here. Although I'm going higher, the sun isn't. A family from New Jersey stops to take pictures with me, but what I really want is to put the bike in their minivan and call it a day. Exhaustion melts into desperation. When will this end? A line of cars drives for the north exit. I make no effort to cling to the edge of the road. Let them go around me. They have a gas pedal.

Three hours after meeting Reed and Lucy, I reach Belle. The campground is ensconced among smooth boulders the color of sand and the height of houses. Joshua trees dot the landscape, their stunted limbs twisting skyward for salvation. All eighteen campsites are taken, but I must crash here. I don't have a choice. With a bicycle and tent I can fit anywhere, and the Mojave Desert has plenty of vacancies. I set up camp in between boulders to shelter myself from the wind and take a last look at the deep blue sky.

Inside the tent, my breath looks like I'm smoking a pack of cigarettes all at once. My middle toes are already frozen and the sun hasn't even set. When it does, the stars sparkle free of light pollution. I see Mercury and Orion from the tent's plastic window. Then I hear laughter and cans being crushed. It must be the band of bros at the next campsite. Their big-wheeled Wrangler was pimped with firewood on the roof and gas canisters on the back bumper. A Jeep, that's how to travel in the desert, not a shared bike pulling a little trailer.

I'm not going outside to stargaze or socialize. The cold is too cold. I'm 800 feet higher than last night. I eat handfuls of dry cereal for dinner. There's still no cell signal, so I can't even check the temperature. I feel my body heat escaping so I put on everything at once. Three T-shirts, a polyester half-zip, and a Brooklyn Industries hoodie. The bait and tackle shop hoodie fits over everything—XXL is the perfect size now. Tomorrow's underwear is on my head tonight. I pull the Walmart sleeping bag over my head and contort my body. The warmest position is kneeling with my chest against my thighs and head tucked between the knees. Arms hug my legs and hands clasp the toes. This might have a name in yoga, but I'm calling it desert survival pose.

A full moon wakes me at two in the morning. The shine is extra bright out here. The sun won't take its place for almost five hours. I'm not sure my feet can wait that long. I go back into desert survival pose.

By eight o'clock it's finally warm enough to step outside. It's been fifteen hours since I crawled into that tent with nothing to do but wait for the next day. I notice my fingernails are dirty and pull out wet wipes to clean them, but the wipes are frozen. My metal water bottle, which I kept next to me overnight, rattles with ice cubes.

CHAPTER 27

HIGHWAY THROUGH HELL

It's a new day and I'm ready for a change. I've been sleeping outdoors in freezing temps for three nights in a row. No showers or hot food. Just dry cereal, peanut butter, bruised fruit, and Hoser's leftover Christmas cookies. I would give my rear wheel for a bowl of Manhattan clam chowder. Without cell service, I haven't heard from the outside world, although I've talked to plenty of visitors curious to know where I parked my car.

The morning sky matches the blue of the bike as I walk it along the sandy campground road. I'm feeling hopeful that by sunset I'll once again know the pleasure of a motel mattress.

"Hey, Citi Bike! Is that really a Citi Bike?" shouts a woman. Jessica and Mason are lounging like lizards on tailgating chairs in hunter orange beanies and polarized sunglasses. They're having a morning bowl (not cereal) and making coffee on a mini propane stove.

A black pitbull named Deus (as in *ex machina*) waits for breakfast until seeing something tastier. He sizes me up, licks his snout, and makes a move. With the grip of a boa constrictor, he humps my leg with rigid passion. His strength is terrifying.

Mason rushes over to pry Deus's legs off my paralyzed thigh. I've never been loved like that before.

The couple can't believe their eyes. They used to live in Greenpoint, Brooklyn. I share my story of why I left New York and every word resonates. They felt the same way and left too. Now living in Venice, Jessica struggles to make commission as a sales rep for a hard cider startup while Mason works remotely for a software company.

Some of their complaints about Brooklyn have resurfaced on the West Coast. They love the California lifestyle, but say that Venice is getting too crowded and pricey. The beauty of the high desert enchants them. Out here they want to build a Binishell, a domed home made by pouring concrete over an inflatable bubble.

Their earthy brown '81 VW bus is parked at the campsite. Mason sympathizes with how I've felt because their engine wheezes climbing these infinity hills. They pass around another bowl, which I decline or else I'll be wheezing too. The next four miles are uphill before I can go down. That's if I ever leave. We've been talking for an hour. I could stay the whole day if I don't cut myself off. We exchange contact information and promise to meet again.

"You're such an inspiration. See you in Venice!" Jessica sings as I roll away.

I've been so pressed to get to campgrounds before dark that I haven't done any side hikes. I would love to come back in a car with the time and energy to explore. When biking across the country, the last thing you want is to add miles, even on foot.

I make one exception. It's for a giant boulder enclosure at Hidden Valley where stolen cattle got rebranded. The mile loop is crowded—with people, not livestock—but walking is a nice change of pace. I overhear a guy who lives in Brooklyn speculating to a friend that the park must have bike share. "Otherwise, there's no way that thing could get here. I mean, it can't leave New York."

I bite my tongue; I don't have time to tell him the truth. The shadows are growing. After a happy walk around Hidden Valley, I've gotta get out of the park. Around here, Joshua trees dot the desert like green cello frill toothpicks dropped from the sky. I feel sorry for them. They have to stay outside all the time. A real bed in a heated room awaits me tonight.

At the same time, now that civilization is within reach, I'm less excited about it. Although I almost got frostbite overnight, I endured to see daylight the next morning. LA isn't far and the journey is almost over. No more camping. No more starry nights. No more alone in nature. No more feeling at peace in a lunar landscape that blew my mind and froze my feet. It's been a hard day's night, but I've explored a National Park and made a few friends doing it.

My phone buzzes back to life. I have a grand total of one text message and it's for 20 percent off at Bed Bath & Beyond. Being plugged in is so overrated. At the park's west exit, I wait behind a river of red taillights, resisting the urge to jump ahead on a bicycle. When it's my turn, the ranger gives me a strange look and waves me through without asking for my pass.

The descent into the town of Joshua Tree is so steep that I ride the brake. Houses have sandy backyards with chain-link fences that make these Joshua trees look like starving prisoners compared to those in the open desert. I declare victory in the parking lot of Safari Motor Inn. It's nothing fancy but I don't care. I can almost feel that hot shower.

As I reach for the door handle, a handwritten sign stops me cold. I stand there. Frozen. Speaking through the gated security door, the Indian motel owner confirms that all rooms are booked for New Year's Eve, which is tomorrow.

"What! You have nothing?" I cry, thinking this must be his

luckiest day in years. "Whatever then, I'll go to the hotel down the street."

"No, no. Booked full. No rooms in town. All gone."

He's gotta be shitting me. Why would people drive to a desert to spend a festive midnight?

"You go to Motel 6 in Twentynine Palms," he orders, referring to a city known for its Marine Corps base. "They have rooms there."

Twentynine Palms is thirteen miles and 30,000 palms in the wrong direction. I feel the cold creeping in with the shadows. It's happening again. It's getting dark and I have no place to stay.

I'm shaking as I approach San Bernardino County Fire Station #36. I've never rung the doorbell at a fire station. Does someone really answer? Sure enough, a man opens the door. I explain the situation, asking to camp in their gated lot where one lonely car is parked. Of course, that's not my end game. I'm fishing for an invitation to sleep on the floor next to the big trucks. I'll join the guys for bowls of chili and cans of beer. I'll hear their crazy stories and they'll hear mine. The next morning I'll roll out with a new T-shirt and more Facebook friends.

"No. I can't let you," he says flatly, citing liability, that legal buzzword that kills any chance to negotiate.

I'm only asking to sleep outside, but he won't have it. He tells me to go to Yucca Valley six miles west. I plead that I can't make it before dark. He's sure that I can if I "hustle" and closes the door in my face.

I push the bike uphill ten blocks to a road marked as a future bike route on Google Maps. The future is not now. After a block, the shoulder turns to sand. I'm forced into the two-lane road, which is a backdoor between Joshua Tree and Yucca Valley that avoids Twentynine Palms Highway, one of California's deadliest roads. This doesn't seem any safer during rush hour with sun glare. Cars must pass me by going into oncoming traffic. I feel their frustration building behind me but hold my ground. If I weren't so exhausted, I'd be scared shitless.

What seems like three weeks later, the shoulder briefly reappears, but is blocked by two cars with hazards flashing. A driver gets out and jogs over. He lives in Brooklyn and heard about a Citi Bike on the loose in California. He says all the campsites and hotels around J-Tree are full, so he and his friends are staying in Indio and taking day trips into the park over the holiday. Another guy gets out and comes over to give me a high five.

"Dude, I can't believe you're on a Citi Bike in Cali! What the what? That's wild! How'd you do it?"

I don't want to talk about it. The sun is down and I'm tired, cold, and hungry. The Safari was full, the firefighter was mean, and this road sucks. Nothing's going my way and now he's standing in it.

"Sorry dude. Well man, I don't wanna hold you up no more, just wanted to stop and say hi," he apologizes before roaring back with confidence. "I never do this, but can we...like...take a selfie?"

I wake up before sunrise on January 1 at the motel the firefighter told me about. The walls are seasick green and the duvet is the color of dried blood. I think I missed it. I fell asleep before midnight holding a bag of SkinnyPop and a bunch of red grapes. A bottle of craft beer sits unopened in the mini fridge. Too late to celebrate? I push the food onto the floor. Nobody parties like I do, I say to myself as I stagger out of bed and reach for the mouthwash.

After fighting up hills through Joshua Tree, I'm ready for downhill rewards to Palm Springs. I'll reenter society by sipping fancy cocktails in hot tubs and whatever else rich people do. The only way to get there is through the Morongo Valley on

Twentynine Palms Highway. I don't know it at the time, but this is one of California's deadliest roads. *The Desert Sun*'s investigative report "Death Trap" found that 182 people were killed over ten years, even more than on a different road called "The Killer Highway."

I crest a final incline and pause to look at the valley below, ignorant of the dangers that await. Concrete safety barriers divide a highway that looks like a strip of bacon frying between desert mountains. Big yellow signs warn Watch Your Speed and Trucks Use Low Gear. For bicycles I would add Extreme Gravity Ahead. Prepare to Woo-Hoo!

I rock forward and exhale. My feet snuggle into the toe guards. I'm spinning so fast I tap the brakes to get more reaction time to avoid rocks and exploded tire treads. Otherwise, the shoulder is comfortable, almost as wide as the travel lane where cars rush past. I'm having so much fun, I'm giddy; my smile can't get any wider.

The road flattens into an intermission. An old blue SUV rolls onto the shoulder in front of me. The two bikes on top tell me this will be a friendly encounter and not another fist to the face. Xander and Marissa hop out. They're a young couple heading to make repairs on their cabin near Joshua Tree, but they turned around when they saw the Citi Bike they had read about. We trade stories about biking and they give me Trader Joe's coconut water and vegan tamales.

I ask about the road ahead and they say it's another steep drop. What they don't say is that the shoulder, previously wide and smooth, narrows and fractures. Puncturevine grows in the cracks. This road literally has thorns. I need to take a travel lane, but the curves through the canyon block visibility for drivers shaking off New Year's Eve hangovers. The last thing they expect around the bend is a bicycle.

But there I am. Traffic zooms around me at raceway speed.

I see a turnout and pull over to pinch myself. Is this really happening? For the next three miles, cars, trucks, and RVs come at me like marbles down a spiral. I am Indiana Jones escaping the booby-trapped Morongo Valley on a bike.

At the Riverside County line I swerve into the other lane to avoid some rocks. At this speed, catching even a small stone could be an instant disaster. The trailer could flip and take the bike down with it, turning me into roadkill. My eyes dart between the road ahead and the traffic behind. Danger is everywhere. From a helmet mirror I watch cars signal into the left lane. A red pickup truck with equipment racks refuses to change course. It's coming up behind me and I can't move right. It's a wall of rock. There's not enough room for both of us in this lane. A tango of terror begins. My heart is pounding. The engine is roaring. I close my eyes.

"HO-LEE-SHIT!" I scream as bike wheels bounce hard across the rumble strip. I skid to a stop on the shoulder that magically appeared just as the canyon walls widened. I need a drink, something stronger than my go-to chocolate milkshake.

I turn onto North Indian Canyon Drive. This will take me south into Palm Springs. The shoulder is sand, but the road is flat and empty. Ahead, I see another bicycle and feel safe again. A senior cyclist pedals toward Twentynine Palms Highway and me. I want to scream, "Stop! Don't go that way!" but he's geared like he knows what he's doing. Sure enough, he turns around and catches up to me.

His name is Phil. To my surprise he's from White Plains, the city next to where I grew up. He says cycling has been part of his life since he and his sister rode their bikes to school. On their way home one day in the 1950s, his mother picked them up in a cab. She told them to leave their bikes on the side of the road. They weren't going home. They flew to California on a propeller plane and he's been here ever since.

I'm trying to absorb this stranger's story on the desert roadside. I used to walk home from elementary school. I can't imagine being uprooted like that. I tell Phil why I left NYC and he picks up on how I'm looking for something else. He also "got tired of being sick and tired" and felt like "a ship without a rudder." He turned to drugs, but then let the Lord Jesus Christ into his heart and it cleansed him. He wishes me luck, saying he and his wife will pray for me tonight.

I thank him and shift my thoughts to Palm Springs and what comes next. All I've heard about this place is golf, cocktail parties, and hot tubs full of men. Back in New York, my event planner coworkers drooled when they spoke of Palm Springs. One even married his partner here and bought a house. I thought Palm Springs was in Florida until planning my route out of Joshua Tree.

Palm Springs doesn't have any Warm Showers hosts. I stay at Motel 6, the cheapest sleep in a pricey place. I walk the main drag looking for my next meal while listening to laughter echo from restaurant patios. It's sad eating by myself with only a laptop for company. I don't play golf and didn't pack any nice clothes to be part of the scene. I don't belong here. This fancy adult playground is not my idea of fun, but I must admit, it sure is pretty. Even the palm trees look elite. Pencil-straight trunks with trimmed tops radiate perfection. Bare mountain walls add soaring dimension to this desert Shangri-La.

My favorite part of Palm Springs is leaving. I weave through quiet streets with mid-century modern homes. Rock gardens with spiky plants surround these houses with flat roofs. Just the hubcaps of cars in the gated driveways surpass my net worth. Maybe someday luxury will call my name, but for now I'm ready to move on.

I pedal from Palm Springs toward an army of wind turbines. White guardians of the beige desert, their chopping arms look ready to blow me back to Arizona. But today the "devil winds" are in my favor. The Santa Anas push me west along State Route 111 until it gets swallowed by the interstate, an eight-lane monster crawling with cars. I'm funneled onto the I-10 with nowhere to hide. The panic ends when I take the next exit just a third of a mile later and follow back roads to the citrus-growing city of Redlands. At fifty miles, today is my last long day, and sure enough, I run out of light.

I call ahead to my host who is a pastor with a lovely wife, four energetic kids, and a black dog named Shadow. They live on a ten-acre orange grove. Dinner is in the works and more fruit than I can imagine is ripe for picking. I fly down a 6 percent grade at dusk. Rounding a final curve, pinpoint lights across the valley come into view like the end of a Hollywood movie. The California of my dreams twinkles ahead.

CHAPTER 28

THE SUN IS SHINING

Los Angeles County

Before the wealthy flocked to Palm Springs, they relaxed in Redlands. In the early 1900s, "The City of Millionaires" was favored for its healthy climate and endless orange orchards. Juicy Redlands is the perfect antidote to the bone dry Southwest and fried food of the Midwest. I stay for eight days. I'm in no hurry. The Pacific Ocean is ninety-nine miles away, an easy roll along bike lanes and trails.

After two nights in a camper van parked in the pastor's orange grove, I move across town. Marcy and her husband are a retired couple who love tandem biking. The backyard of their historic brick home is paradise for my taste buds. Avocados, lemons, key limes, oro blanco grapefruits, and navel oranges are hanging from trees. Wooden name tags are nailed to the trunks. I apologize to Momma, Omega, and Patty O as I pull fruit from their branches and run inside like a squirrel hoarding nuts.

Marcy is doing the dishes in a blue turtleneck and white apron. A plate with what looks like distressed tomatoes sits on the counter.

"What's that?" I ask.

"Ah, that's a persimmon," she says above the running water. "Our one tree probably yields 400 persimmons. We have so many that the branches broke! I scoop out their insides when soft and soupy," she says, demonstrating over the sink. "They taste like sugar. My house specialty is to add the pulp to my key lime margarita mix. It's very nice. You don't need the triple sec if you do that."

Marcy connects me to her friend Mark Friis, a heal-the-world type with mountain man features. His sinewy frame carries an emotional burden. Over the years Mark has been a contractor and cabinet maker, bike shop mechanic and competitive racer. His wife's job in mapping software brought them to Redlands. One day while walking the dog, she was hit by a driver who had fallen asleep. She wound up in the ICU; he didn't even get a ticket. There was no advocate for pedestrians or bicyclists in the area. After an off-duty cop killed a rider in Mark's bike club while texting and driving, he organized a memorial ride and 400 cyclists showed up.

"Someone came up to me and said, 'Whatever you did here, you can't let it end here,'" he recalls. "You know that quote, 'Be the change you want to see in the world'? Well, I took it to heart and ran with it."

Mark quit his job and started the nonprofit Inland Empire Biking Alliance for Riverside and San Bernardino counties.

We're having sandwiches on the patio of a small eatery chatting about his journey through life and my journey through America.

"I like the idea of losing everything and starting over," he says about my trip. "When you've done that and reinvented yourself, it's exciting. You can restart your own life."

In the distance, powder-white peaks of the San Bernardino Mountains contrast with the palm trees lining Olive Avenue with its stately homes in eclectic styles. Our phones are on the table. Mark's device lights up with a text. Then another. More pinging. Now ringing. Mark ignores all of it and looks at me with watery eyes.

"Somebody's dead."

"He got the left hook," Mark tells me the next day. A thirty-three-year-old cyclist was sailing down a hill and collided with a left-turning driver, age ninety-two. We pay tribute by placing a ghost bike at the intersection in Loma Linda, the town next door. Spray painted white, ghost bikes memorialize a bicyclist fatality. The tradition started in St. Louis in 2003.

"This city is so anti-bike," Mark says with a frown. "Loma Linda doesn't give a crap. It would not surprise me at all if this was removed by the end of the day. It's bringing attention to them they don't like."

The victim's girlfriend gets out of her car and runs to Mark, who is locking the ghost bike to a stop sign. Sobbing, she throws her arms around him. I stand back with hands clasped, unsure of what to do, and then follow Mark back to his Prius.

Mark has known seven cyclists killed by cars over the years; three of them were good friends. Being the only outlet for bicycle grief across two counties has taken an emotional toll. "The one line I don't cross is I don't go to funerals for people I don't know," he says. "I wind up making speeches and answering questions. Our common thing is that someone died. I don't want to make friends out of a tragedy, but I will help with legal reports and things like that." He pauses and looks at me. "If not me, then who?"

I ride through Claremont, "City of Trees & PhDs," and Pomona, "a sunny place for shady people," jokes my host Demi who turned his hobby of biking into a delivery business. He rides with me to The Donut Man on Route 66 in Glendora where we eat tiger tails and lemon-filled pastries. I pedal through Azusa—"A to Z in the USA" joked comedian Jack Benny—and spend a night in Monrovia, home of Trader Joe's corporate. Arrival in Pasadena gets the attention of my college friend Miell. "Get Korean food in Pasadena, Jeffrey! It makes 32nd Street look like white people food," she writes, referring to K-Town in Manhattan where we've shared meals.

Caltech Bike Lab organizes a ride in my honor to Eagle Rock Brewery via the Arroyo Seco bike path. I'm now socializing in northeast Los Angeles but leave the city after a few beers. A hand-drawn "Welcome Countri Bike" poster greets me in Glendale. My host Melanie read a story about me on LAist.com and reached out to offer her place for a night. Over a backyard fire pit we watch a Democratic primary debate on a projection screen, cheering Bernie and laughing when the flames cast a shadow on Hillary.

The next day I enter the City of Angels for real. My first host Mikey lives in Silver Lake. He's a competitive racer living with a bike buddy roommate. I'm not sure what Mikey does for work. All his Warm Showers profile says is "full-time danger boy." He rides hard and parties harder, judging from the pot paraphernalia strewn across the living room. After a bowl at Silverlake Ramen, we join a group ride over the historic Sixth Street Bridge that will be demolished next week for fears it could collapse in an earthquake. In the morning I wake up on the couch to the hiss of a butane torch lighting a bong.

Hating on LA has a rich tradition, but then you miss the magic. With an open mind I find that I really like it here. I breeze along bike lanes free of traffic congestion. Drivers often yield their right-of-way. Unlike impatient New Yorkers, a short delay doesn't break LA's day. Angelenos were born to sit in gridlock; the average resident wastes five days a year commuting to work.

I zip between neighborhoods and bounce around with different hosts. My newest friend is Greg, a climate-driven cyclist who works for bicycle rack maker Dero. His uncle makes the New Year's Eve confetti that is hand-tossed over Times Square, so Greg has spent time in both cities.

"LA gets a bad rap for having so many assholes, which there are, but if you get out of your car and talk to your neighbor, it's a really cool city," he says.

By now the word is out. A Citi Bike crossed America. I'm invited to the towering headquarters of LA's transportation authority above Union Station. I meet the leaders of Metro Bike Share that will launch soon. I test ride a prototype, which feels like a Cadillac compared to my Citi clunker. A group of us enjoy a sushi lunch in Little Tokyo and meet up at a brewery that night.

The alternative transportation movement is a great way to meet people. I follow my new bike friends to the opening of The Wheelhouse in the Arts District. I meet Tami who quit her job to open this bike and coffee clubhouse where anyone is welcome. Downstairs is a coffee shop, and the loft is a bike and mechanic shop. She says it's an experiment in building community. The crowd is radiating good vibes. I get placemaking inspiration on how I want to make an impact on my future community. For now though, I call it a night, my last in LA. It's time to move on. I'm actually not quite done. There is one more city to go.

Santa Monica's Breeze Bike Share creates an East Meets West group ride for the grand finale. Saturday begins with Dinosaur

Coffee at Sunset and Fountain. Greg is there and I meet Nick Richert, the host of the radio podcast *Bike Talk*. Nick wants to ride along and record the ending of this historic trip. Ironically, the day is also historic on the opposite coast. A blizzard dumps a record amount of snow on NYC and completely shuts down Citi Bike. Only one bike is still in operation, and it's heading to a beach 3,000 miles from those impassable roads.

Greg leads the way along the Sunset Boulevard bike lane through Hollywood. We drop down to Santa Monica Boulevard and cross into WeHo where the brunch scene is at full volume. The bike lane ends, unsurprisingly, at the border of Beverly Hills, so we take parallel side roads and then pass through Century City and West LA before hitting Santa Monica.

The rendezvous point is in a park. A few riders on green Breeze bikes are already here. Santa Monica Breeze is the first, and so far only, bike share system among the eighty-eight cities in LA county. Joshua Tree friends Jessica and Mason arrive, as do cyclists I don't know on bikes fast and slow. Even the former mayor, ever the politician, joins the action. I'm told that if there's a camera or microphone he'll be next to it. Bicyclists are making new connections and the *esprit de corps* is palpable. We roll from the park toward the pier just two miles away.

For the final countdown, my mind backpedals. I have a lot of memories, especially about food and people, even those I met for only a few minutes. Like that cashier who caught my eye and gave me the perfect chocolate shake leaving Pittsburgh. Dawn the Cincinnati photographer with her amazing zucchini bread. Louisville BBQ and bourbon with Beth and Forrest. The elderly farmer in Ashley, Illinois, who stopped his truck to give me red peppers and tomatoes. A host in St. Louis who gave me lavender honey made by bees in her backyard.

As a male, I was fortunate not to worry about unwanted advances while sleeping in someone's home. As a white male, I didn't fear a police response just for being a stranger in a small town. Yet even privileged white men are not immune to violence, as I found out bloodied on a rural road outside Tulsa.

Being on a bicycle increases your vulnerability, but lets you tap into a community with tremendous resources. Cycling creates bonds stronger than running clubs and CrossFit gyms. The Warm Showers network opens homes to two-wheeled travelers across the country and around the world.

I also remember those who gave me support at critical junctures. Bike shop mechanics like Saul in DC and the Indiana DOT boss who let me pass on a closed road so I didn't detour uphill. Oklahomans like Haskell, who welcomed me at a cafe after my one and only flat, and Meagan the Tulsa TV reporter who kept in touch. And Tom and Linda, my hitchhiker heroes in windswept New Mexico.

As an introvert, though, perhaps my favorite memories were just-me-in-nature moments. A buggy August afternoon on the C&O Canal wearing an American flag bandana in my hair, a dirty white T-shirt, and a bright white smile. Months later on the Katy Trail surrounded by fall foliage while reading signs about Lewis and Clark and listening to birds who had so much to say. I had never camped before, but enjoyed making a temporary nest outside and waking up at daybreak to move somewhere new.

The journey was not without hardship. I was punched in the face by an axe murderer in Oklahoma. I kept going. Relentless wind pummeled me in New Mexico. I kept going. I ran out of water in rural Missouri. I ran out of warmth in snowy Arizona and Joshua Tree National Park. I kept going. I kept going because the new reality I was discovering, although painful at times, was more fulfilling than the status quo I left behind at my Manhattan desk. Rolling into the unknown felt like progress, rather than staying put with a career and city I knew weren't working for me. I left a life good enough to find something better. I dismissed stereotypes of places I had never been to see them for myself. I broke the rules of bike sharing, but I paid my dues for the chance to experience America on my terms, meet inspirational people, and maybe inspire them too.

Up ahead the palm trees break and the sun reflects like a mirror. The Pacific Ocean. My jaw stiffens. I actually finished this thing. Biking 37.4 miles here and 45.8 miles there added up to 3,020 miles from midtown Manhattan to the Santa Monica Pier.

We take group photos with our bikes and the pier's iconic blue and white arch in the background. Ocean Avenue is busy and it's hard to get a good shot. Cars get in the way. Tourists get in the way. The former mayor gets in the way. Enough, I'm ready to start our handlebar happy hour. We head to the beachfront Ristorante Al Mare. I say I'll meet the group there. I just want to finish this how I started, alone and with discomfort about what comes next.

Route 66 pavement ends at a stop sign with blinking red lights. I walk the bike on wooden planks past the arcade and amusement park to the end of the pier. Facing the ocean, I lean over the railing and close my eyes to the warming sun. The end is here but so is the beginning. I am alone again, now all the way west.

CHAPTER 29

NEW BEGINNING IN THE MIDDLE OF AMERICA

Making it to California gets renewed attention from the *New York Post* and NBC New York, both of which covered me four months ago in Pittsburgh. *People* runs the article, "Man Set to Finish His Cross Country Ride on Shared Citi Bike (And Yes, He Plans on Returning It)."

Most people reacted with awe or congratulations. Some thought the whole idea was really stupid; only a fool would pay so much for that bike. And a handful of haters were furious. A blogger in Brooklyn wrote, "He should have been met at the California border by the NYPD, not NBC." In response to my comment on NBC that "I've spent enough time on this bicycle—it's someone else's turn. I'm happy to return it to the bike sharing system," the blogger fumed, "Yeah, no shit. It was actually someone else's turn to ride the bike four months and forty-five minutes ago." For good measure, he signed off with #crime, #citibike, #selfishness, #tragedyofthecommons.

Returning it was the plan, but while in LA I meet someone who used to work at Citi Bike corporate. After backchanneling, she reports they want nothing to do with me. They won't give even a partial refund. Instead, they will strip off all my stickers as if none of this ever happened.

"Don't do it! That bike belongs in a museum!" cries a follower on Instagram. My small but engaged audience is totally opposed to giving back the bike that I paid for. The executive officer of active transportation and sustainability at Metro wants to buy Countri Bike and hang it in his art gallery downtown. In the end, Breeze Bike Share ships it home on their tab. However, I'm a nomad with no physical address, only a post office box that won't accept a bike. Luckily, I'm still friendly with the super of my old Brooklyn apartment building, so we send it to him.

Lounging on Venice Beach in January, I'm in no rush to return to winter in New York. That is, until I get an email from a producer at *The Late Show with Stephen Colbert*. Goodbye, Pacific Ocean.

The show pays for my flight and to express ship the bike. Since I don't have anywhere to stay, they also pay for two nights at Le Parker Meridien. My parents drive down from Vermont and my sister takes the train from Boston. We squish together in one room like on a childhood family trip. To the taping I also invite David, the Australian photographer I hired pre-trip. My parents sit in the audience while my sister and David join me in a private green room stocked with snacks and swag. The bike is with us, too. No reason to return it. Colbert wants to see it more than Citi Bike does. I drink a Bronx Brewery pale ale to calm my nerves.

A producer comes into the room with bad news. The show "overbooked the talent" and needs to cut a segment. Mine. They'll tape my interview, but won't air it tonight. Not to worry, the producer says. Richard Dreyfuss was cut last night and will be added to an episode next week.

Disappointment runs deeper when I find out why. The show

needs to create a skit around its sponsor Mini Cooper. A car is bumping my story that I hoped would inspire viewers to incorporate a bike into their lives for a little more happiness.

The taping is going too long. Stephen is tired. The crew is frustrated. The audience is hungry. I am the last order of business. They are still going to tape me, but it's a one-shot deal. No take twos. Plenty could go wrong, even before I open my mouth. I must ride the bike onto the set, cleanly dismount, flip the kickstand, and not trip on the two steps leading to the armchair. The pressure is on. I know Colbert will dominate the interview, but I have one line to get across. I rehearse it for an hour in the green room in between sips of beer.

"The best part of my job was my bike commute, so I quit the job and I—" before I can finish with "kept commuting," Colbert interrupts, "What was the job...that was so desperately terrible that *this* was an improvement?"

The interview is a blur. It felt like being in the driver's seat with someone else at the controls. Colbert is a professional comedian, but I do land one joke of my own.

Colbert: "Are your legs like oak now? Can I feel your calves?"

Me, startled: Lifts one leg.

Colbert, reaching over the desk to squeeze my calves: "Not that great, I gotta say."

Audience: Laughter.

Me: "Actually, if you felt this part (slapping my butt), this is the strongest part!"

Colbert, sitting down: "Ah hah...I'm...I'm. I'm good."

The audience roars, but the segment never airs. Millions of viewers never hear my story. Some would have contacted me. Maybe I would get a book deal, job offer, or marriage proposal. It should have been the launching pad to the next chapter of my life. Instead, the silver lining to flirting with fame is the memories made from our spontaneous family gathering. Back in the green room, David secretly took a video of the TV screen showing the live taping, giving me a record of a bittersweet end to a wild ride.

Six months after meeting Colbert, I say goodbye to NYC. This time it's for good. I close my post office box in Chinatown and clean out the storage unit in Brooklyn. I drive a yellow Penske truck across the blue Manhattan Bridge that I biked over countless times like it was no big deal.

Driving on the bridge for the first time marks the end of an era. My parents, grandparents, and great grandparents lived in New York. We've been New Yorkers since immigrating from Eastern Europe in the late 1800s. My parents retired to Vermont and my sister stayed in Boston after college. The rest of the immediate family is underground. Within the hour, the last living root of our family tree will be pulled from the Empire State.

I'm heading west again, but this time much faster. I take a victory lap at familiar places. I spend a weekend with Val in Pittsburgh that coincides with OpenStreetsPGH. I ride Countri Bike and reconnect with Pittsburgh pedalers like Dan and Kieran. I drive down the West Virginia Panhandle and stop for a shake at Howdy's Dari-Owl near Wheeling, just as I had on the bike en route to a creepy hilltop lodge. This time I skip that and stay with cousins in Cincinnati.

After a good night's sleep I grab lunch at New Albanian Brewing Company, near Louisville, where on the bike I detoured for a pint too many. When I walk in, the manager smiles and says, "Countri Bike?" like I was here last week. Back in the charming Katy Trail town of Hermann, I enjoy another German dinner at the winery and sleep in the truck parked outside.

The next day I'm driving just south of the Kansas state line. The road curves out of sight. "There's gonna be a Dollar General," I say to myself. Around the bend, the discount store appears. "Dollar General, the only general I take orders from!" I yell with a hand-to-forehead salute.

I laugh so hard at my inside joke that I almost drive off the road. I flash back ten months ago sitting there with a candy bar. The sun was high as I rested with my Citi Bike in the middle of a parking lot in the middle of America. I had nowhere to be and no one to answer to, except maybe the Dollar General himself.

I continue driving on Route 66. Approaching Claremore, I remember the butterflies in my stomach acting like bees. I was bicycling on a four-lane highway and praying everyone would move over because I couldn't. I was riding next to semis and there was no fucking shoulder.

"What the hell is he doing?" I ask myself as I change lanes to pass the me that's no longer there. I'm in the driver's seat now, about forty miles from Tulsa. I'll be there before dark.

Tomorrow I start a lease that's 70 percent less than what I was paying in Brooklyn. Hooray for savings, but the so-called buckle of the Bible Belt is not where Jewish boys born on the Upper East Side move at midlife. I'm going from the Empire State to one whose license plates sloganize mediocrity: "Oklahoma is OK."

I had other options. Pittsburgh delighted me with its bicycle culture, steel bridges, and gritty spirit. Cincinnati wowed me with breweries and historic buildings begging for renovation. And I'll never forget moaning over barbecue in St. Louis, home to stunning parks and museums. These cities have professional sports, boutique hotels, bike lanes, craft breweries, and decent ethnic food. But enough East and West Coast expats already live there.

Tulsa has almost none of the above in 2016. There's not even a convenience store downtown. The urban renaissance elsewhere is far ahead of Tulsa, and I kinda like that. I'm ready for a fresh start in a place that needs me as much as I need it. The former Oil Capital of the World needs a new engine, one fueled by startups and placemaking concepts. I have no job, but come with a business dream of my own. I don't know how it will go, but the chance to succeed is better than being trapped at my desk in New York. I would still be there if I hadn't turned my bike commute into a cross-country quest to see what else was out there.

Oklahoma? OK! The time is right for Tulsa and for me. Together we will help each other. Tulsans are supportive and accessible. They're born huggers. They're about collaboration, not competition. It's not about being a big fish in a small pond, but being in the right pond.

Exactly one year after taking the bike on a ferry to New Jersey, I receive the keys to a studio apartment in downtown Tulsa. Rent is $650. The renovated brick building once housed oil workers in the 1920s. Everyone in Oklahoma has a car, but not me. I save money and get around on my old Raleigh road bike. Every two weeks I pedal four miles to Trader Joe's and four miles home with forty pounds of groceries on my back. The Citi Bike ends up in a transportation exhibit at the Tulsa Historical Society.

Here it's easy to volunteer, join committees, and make new friends. Ultimately, I want to start my own business. I sense opportunity in this city thirsty for ideas. I have a passion project to create a social space for travelers. I don't have the money or experience, but then again, I had never bicycled beyond NYC before pedaling to LA.

In the meantime, I network and look for jobs. Tulsa has a number of creative agencies. I get information interviews, but they don't lead to anything. Month after month, I am losing money. Freelance writing isn't enough. Royalties from the app, which once paid rent in Brooklyn, now don't even cover housing here. I become a minimalist to the max. I skip meals. Switch to a cheaper cell carrier. Cancel my internet.

In bed I stare at the cracks from water damage on the ceiling, wondering what to do. Will I let disappointment drive me back east or farther west? I've struggled with this rudderless feeling before. It's what led me to become a bike nomad, but I can't run the same play again. On hot summer nights I leave the AC off and let the ceiling fan hypnotize me. The blades spin like a wheel of fortune.

I widen my job search, applying to coordinate events at Margaritaville and move rental cars around the airport. By now I haven't had a regular paycheck in three and a half years. I'm down to a few hundred dollars and hanging on by my fingernails. I start part time at the Gap in Utica Square. Folding slim fit dress shirts for ten bucks an hour wasn't what I expected when I moved here a year ago.

Finally, a break. I'm hired as a senior content specialist at ConsumerAffairs, a reviews website that's a resource for buyers and a lead generator for brands. I walk seven minutes to work or ride in two; there's a bike room in the lobby. The penthouse office has windows and balconies on all sides. Free snacks. Bacon Friday breakfasts. Fridges stocked with LaCroix, iced tea, and beer. Kombucha and nitro coffee flow on tap. Coworkers are friendly. The day starts at nine and ends at five; nobody stays late. We work remotely one day a week and have unlimited PTO. Every two weeks, salary is deposited like magic. I am contributing to something exciting and feel alive with purpose.

A year later I'm promoted to managing editor. I bank every available dollar to invest in my own projects like starting a walking tour company downtown. Just like feeling on cloud nine after getting my dream job in NYC, I am floating on top of Tulsa.

When coronavirus first hit the US, I felt secure. We already knew how to work remotely and our editorial team has been "crushing it." A company-wide presentation reassures us they had been planning for a downturn in business and are ready to weather the pandemic. I approach my two-year job anniversary with pride and confidence. Two weeks later, on the day my editor team hit its first-quarter goal, I am let go over Zoom.

Alone and unemployed during the lockdown, I double down to move forward on my own. Never again would I trust having job security from someone else. Walking tours could give me an independent path forward, but COVID-19 blocked it. Even with only a few customers, I press ahead to create online content and offer outdoor tours. When space next to a popular coffee shop becomes available, I strike a sweet deal with the landlord.

Five years and five weeks after getting punched in the face outside Tulsa, I open a tour office to promote my adopted hometown. My storefront on South Boston Avenue is the Broadway of Tulsa. The building is a dazzling art deco landmark from when this was the Oil Capital of the World. I display vintage Oklahoma items hunted down on eBay, my socially distant activity of choice—everything from postcards and pennants to eight-foot Gothic stained-glass church windows.

Tours are only the first part of my hospitality vision. Cashing in savings from my lost job, I plan to lease studios above a brewery once the apartments are renovated. I'll live in one and put the rest on Airbnb, decorating each with an Oklahoma theme. Then I can host road trippers with the same kindness I experienced while traveling. Launching a travel business during a global pandemic isn't the best timing, but I moved to Tulsa to start something meaningful and be my own boss after years of working for others with little to show for it. The opportunity is here and the time is now.

I don't know if these small ventures will succeed. A lot could go wrong. But at least I've unlocked a path toward personal freedom that eluded me in NYC until I hopped on a Citi Bike. I was so hesitant to change gears that I might have stayed in The Grotto or bounced to another event company only to restart the cycle of discontent.

I've gone from giving walking tours of Wall Street in Manhattan to illuminating the plight of Black Wall Street in Tulsa. People move to NYC to chase their dreams. I left to chase mine.

Looking back, crossing America was only the first challenge. Starting up fresh after the spokes stopped spinning required even more endurance. Yet through the good and the bad, right-size Tulsa feels more like home than a megalopolis ever did.

The journey to change my life—which began while Citi Biking to work over the Manhattan Bridge—didn't end when I rolled onto the Santa Monica Pier or opened the door to my own business. I still have many miles to go. Maybe all that riding was just to find the right place for the next chapter to begin.

ACKNOWLEDGMENTS

A long and arduous journey required a lot of support. The first to help was my sister Allison. Our sibling bond let me incubate this idea before telling our parents, who predictably freaked out. Her wise counsel at the outset and invaluable editing at the end gave clarity to my plan and manuscript. This book is dedicated to my parents for their unwavering love and for not dragging me back east after getting punched in the Midwest.

In New York, thank you Patricia Helding for your pre-trip push and sustained support. Keep baking; the country needs your Fat Witch brownies. Thanks to editor Noah Ballard for strengthening the manuscript, and to the publishing team at Scribe Media for keeping me on track. And to my best buddy, Tommy Gonzalez. Who else would let me stash a Citi Bike in their apartment the night before I left, check my mailbox while I was gone, FaceTime me when alone in my tent, and come to Brooklyn in the clutch after the TaskRabbit mover canceled?

I am deeply grateful to those who hosted me for a night or three. Although space limitations prevented me from recounting all of our memories, your hospitality during this vulnerable time was truly cherished. Special thanks to Mark,

Karen, Michelle, and Daniel Grosser for their above-and-beyond hospitality in Cincinnati. I am also indebted to the volunteers behind Warmshowers.org. Without their platform, this trip was not financially or logistically possible. Opening your home to strangers sounds risky, but among bicyclists, it just seems natural.

Additional gratitude to bike shops for their free or discounted services: City Bikes in DC, Tom's Bicycles in Tulsa, and Sun Adventure Sports in Amarillo. High fives to bike sharing mechanics for free tune-ups like Evan in Pittsburgh, Josh in Columbus, and Damian at Citi Bike itself after I returned to NYC. A word to Citi Bike corporate: loosen your helmet—it's on too tight.

To the bike sharing systems and advocacy groups that were open-minded, thanks for the conversations, coffees, and beers. They include HealthyRide and BikePGH in Pittsburgh, CoGo in Columbus, Red Bike and Urban Basin Bicycle Club in Cincinnati, Trailnet in St. Louis, Tulsa Hub, Spokies in OKC, Bici in Albuquerque, Caltech Bike Lab in Pasadena, Metro Bike Share in Los Angeles, and Breeze in Santa Monica.

Also in California, shoutouts to Mark Friis for his deep conversations and indomitable spirit. To Avital Shavit, Julia Salinas, Brett Thomas, and others at Metro; Cuong Phu Trinh and Dustin Foster at Caltrans; Greg Heining at Dero; and Nick Richert of *Bike Talk*. Y'all are great. Keep up the good fight to get people out of cars and onto public transit or #bikeinstead. To Cynthia Rose at Santa Monica Spoke for her East Meets West enthusiasm and coordination. To everyone who showed up at the pier, including Jason Cochran, Greg Brandes, Lara Solomon, Bryan Beretta, Jessica and Mason, and Melanie and Julie, thanks for making the end so memorable.

Support was also virtual. To the Instagram followers, I appreciated encouragement on the windiest days and darkest nights. To name a few: agawag, aldogs10, aomarsmile, ayogist, crownview, ctrl_alt.delete, dawnmurrayphotography, dcwaits, djac2828, elginmccargo, eugenetsang, hthrbeach, imthebraun, indygibble, julie.robortaccio, justing499, katebomma, kevmikeberg, klee088, _kristinl, leawheels, melnarkie, plymouthfury, roadscholars, 5chw4r7z, tiseo.steve. And to those who donated to my ride, thank you.

Hugs to the Tulsans who enriched my relocation, especially Michael Grogan, Matt Williams, Lindsay Hart, Samuel Smith, Sarah Huston Graves, Maggie Brown, Isaac Rocha, Daniel Regan, Jessica Litchfield-Cermak, Patsy Hepner, Ren Barger, Craig Longacre, Josh New, Omar Ghadry, Sandi Griffin, and Maddie Klein. To Price Family Properties for seeing my tourism potential. To Ken Busby for his fact checking and Route 66 stewardship. To Cathy Essley for her enduring friendship from flat tire in Claremore to Gothic windows in Glenpool. And to Soundpony, never change.

Finally, to the curious folks I met in small towns along back roads. Our lives intersected briefly, but your kindness to a stranger was a welcome blessing. Thank you.

ABOUT THE AUTHOR

JEFFREY TANENHAUS is the first person to cross a continent by bike share. The New York native broke away from the rat race to ride a Citi Bike 3,020 miles from Manhattan to Los Angeles. Media coverage of his feat included *People, Forbes, The Guardian, New York Magazine, Newsweek, Condé Nast Traveler*, BBC Travel, Lonely Planet, Mashable, KCRW (NPR), and *The Late Show with Stephen Colbert*. Jeffrey lives in Tulsa with his two bikes.

countribike.com | @countribike

CPSIA information can be obtained
at www.ICGtesting.com
Printed in the USA
LVHW031548271021
701710LV00002B/218